Memoirs of a
Feeble Cabbage

Memoirs of a Feeble Cabbage

A Life In Malaria Research
And Other Adventures

Geoff Butcher

First published 2022 by Dandelion Digital, an imprint of Paper Lion Ltd
13 Grayham Road, New Malden, Surrey, KT3 5HR, UK
www.paperlionltd.com
info@paperlion.co.uk

A catalogue record for this book is available from the British Library

ISBN
Paperback: 978-1-908706-43-0
eBook: 978-1-908706-44-7

Design: cover by Charlie Newhouse, interior by seagulls.net

Cover image of car: adapted from a photo by Andrew Bone, 2017
under cc-by-2.0 licence https://creativecommons.org/licenses/
by/2.0/deed.en
Author photo: Helen Rawlins

For Sue, who taught me the meaning of love

Contents

Back to Business – Malaria 69

One Project Two Bosses 81

WHO Goes Where? 103

Australia 119

Back to UK 135

Reflections on Research 155

Personal Reflections 159

Introduction

"Scientists are rarely to be counted among the fun people.
Awkward at parties, shy with strangers, deficient in irony –
they have had no choice but to turn their attention
to the close study of everyday objects."
Fran Lebowitz 1946– *Metropolitan Life* (1978)

Anyone coming across the above quotation, whether or not they are scientists, may remember someone they met who resembled this characterisation. Recently, the more I thought about it, the more I came to realise the quotation would probably not apply to my colleagues, but it is an accurate description of me as a young man. This was a time when my awkwardness and shyness of strangers, especially at interviews, was a hindrance to my ability to get on with my peers. Looking back, I realise now that I was an isolated child. As in the quotation, to occupy my time at age 10, I devoted increasing hours peering down a microscope, bought surprisingly for ten shillings from a shop in Coalville, Leicestershire. Much to my mother's horror, I dissected worms and insects and anything else I could get hold of, all of which she regarded as dirty and disgusting. But I believe this fascination with the natural world awakened in me an interest in science.

Unsurprisingly, it isn't until you have lived most of your life that you are in a position to analyse the many factors that came together to make you what you are. I was fortunate that although it took twenty years for me to talk to someone who could explain why I was the person I was, their experience enabled me to develop an approach to the various challenges that I had to deal with from early childhood onwards. I hope that in writing this volume that others will find it helpful – and might learn something scientific along the way.

Of course, human behaviour is subject to many influences but most of the men I knew were my uncles or cousins who worked in the coal industry, and this made an impression on me as I sat listening to their stories. I had a vague feeling that unless I passed my exams, I too would be sent down the mines – despite the absence of any in West London, such was my horror of going underground. Lastly, throughout my life I have been considerably underweight and therefore unable to join my contemporaries in games of any sort which contributed to my fear of failure. This left me with time alone with my microscope, regardless of my mother's disapproval. I didn't realise as I was growing up how much physical activity was important, especially to boys, to enable them to make connections with others and in helping to deal with emotional stress.

A life in service

My mother and her sister Kit, left home at 14 to go into service. They were greeted by the driver of a horse and cart, sent to the station to collect them and asked if they had brought their bottles because they looked so young. They worked mostly in the big estates in Derbyshire and surrounding counties. My mother started as a scullery maid in one of the big houses, and blamed all the standing and washing heavy copper pots as the cause of her bunions later in life. One of her memories was of being in an attic bedroom, where servants usually slept, listening to the rats running across the bed.

It wasn't all hard grind though as it seemed they made time to have fun; some of the landed gentry would lay on balls for their servants, including the provision of transport to return them home. They used to play tricks on one another – if one of the footmen got up from the table at dinner, they'd remove his plate and put it underneath, so on return he would put his feet in it. She told one story of how she tried riding a bike which went out of control downhill and ran into a cow – she never rode a bike again!

She eventually became a head cook but, oddly, said she never thought she would be able to 'think for herself', even though she managed to rise up the servant ranks. Amongst others, my mother and her sister worked for Lord and Lady Vernon in Derbyshire, who also had a house in Eaton Square in London. Because it became increasingly difficult for employers to get staff after WWI, my mother found it was fairly easy to go from one estate house to another if she didn't like the conditions – especially if they treated staff as though they were in the army.

My mother's job as head cook, was to see Lady Vernon every morning to decide on the menu for the day. On one particular morning she fainted, was promptly taken to hospital and found to be anaemic, for which the treatment was to eat raw liver. From then on, she was always given a chair to sit on when working out the menu. She worked in quite a few large houses in London, but not necessarily staying in them; she was lent out to organise the larger dinner parties. Servants often moved between different families, especially as they were frequently related to each other. My aunt Kit rose to the rank of lady's maid, which was quite an important position.*

---

* An interesting account of the life of a lady's maid by Rosina Harrison, a maid to Lady Astor, the first woman MP "The Lady's maid my Life in Service".

The Vernons, like others of the landed gentry, also had parties for the young people from London and elsewhere. By all accounts, a rowdy crowd much like the antics written about by PG Woodhouse in the Jeeves and Wooster stories. One of their tricks was to put washing soda crystals in the beds – which wasn't very comfortable to sleep on, assuming you went to sleep. They also broke things, especially crockery – including the potties kept under the bed. Lady Vernon would send Kit to London to buy new "articles" of the same make and design. On their boating lake, one night they overheard Lord Vernon tell someone to "leave his bl***y wife alone". In fact, Lord Vernon (referred to by the staff as 'Lordy'), was not at all an authoritarian figure. Rather than rebuke a servant himself if he saw them doing something wrong, he would ask another servant to correct them.

When the government took over estates during World War II, many servants went to work in factories. Aunt Kit went to work in a factory that made ball bearings. One night, the foreman said to the ladies "you don't have to worry about getting it too precise", but they knew how important it was for the sake of their own men operating the equipment that depended on those bearings. They were so angry with the foreman that they pinned him against the wall and threatened him with dire consequences if he said it again. However, their conscientious work attitude didn't stop them stealing the much sort-after grease-proof paper which they hid in their undergarments, to take home and use for baking cakes.

My mother met my father when he was working for a butcher and he was tasked with settling the accounts for the big houses in London. When servants married, they invariably had to leave service, in case they had children. So, my parents moved to a small flat in Fulham on the Bishop's estate.

How to survive bombs, beatings and boredom

So, my beginning was in September 1940 at the start of the Blitz. I was driven with my mother, despite the air raids, in a London County Council ambulance to Queen Charlotte's Hospital where I made my first appearance and incidentally, where both my children were born years later. The nurses were still scrubbing the floors in the recently opened hospital, presumably to stave off infection.

Our flat in Fulham had no bathroom, so instead we used a tin bath on Friday nights in front of a coal fire. Part of the ritual for me, was being given senna pods to make me go to the toilet. I often had abdominal pain, which I tried to relieve by sitting on the toilet for hours, until one night it got so bad they sent for the doctor and I was whisked off to Fulham hospital in an ambulance. I spent two weeks in hospital following an appendectomy and still bear the scars. They must have run out of surgical twine to sew me up; the scars are so obvious they probably went to Woolworths to get some string. I think I was 14 then and was put in a mens ward*. I was looked after by a very bossy little nurse with whom I was always in trouble, but there was an angel in the form of a catholic nun, who wore the whitest of white habits and she really was an angel, the sort of person you never forget.

In those days, equipment was sterilised on the ward and wrapped in paper. Hypodermic needles had to be cleaned out and resharpened, (not always successfully), so there was something to watch all the time. I'd asked for my microscope and slides to be brought to the ward and an old man wanted to know why I was polishing those "bits of glass", but the next day he had passed away,

---

* This scenario could have been prevented had we known about Dr Burkett's research on the importance of fibre in the diet, something I found out years later.

5

so I missed the opportunity to have a chat and explain to him what I was doing. On a shelf in the men's lavatory there were rows of bottles containing urine samples – varying from light yellow to deep red – waiting to be tested. I assume this would have been for the presence of glucose using 'Fehling's solution', a test we did in 'A level' chemistry, although obviously we used a made-up sugar solution*. I had to return to the hospital after a couple of weeks for the surgeon to check my wound and I asked him if I was fit to play rugby, hoping like anything he was going to say "of course not!" Unfortunately, he said the opposite and that I was fit and ready to go. I was not the only one of our family who bore the scars of an operation. By co-incidence my father had a suspected tubercular lump removed from his thyroid gland under anaesthetic with ether on the kitchen table, aged twelve, in 1915. I have just come across an article by a retired GP who had the same operation, also under ether anaesthetic – but perhaps not on the kitchen table.

My father worked long hours as a milk foreman for the United Dairies, though he had many different jobs before that, including one with Marconi and at one time cleaning up elephant dung in a circus. My mother and I, along with thousands of other Londoners, moved to the country to escape the bombing in WWII, staying with family or friends. My father was in a reserved occupation and was not called up to join the forces, so he stayed in London. My uncle Arthur and aunt Doris had a flat opposite ours in Kenyon Street. Though we all had Anderson shelters in our gardens, on one night we were sheltering together. My father went out to check on what was happing during the air raid and when he came back, in his usual nonchalant manner, he said to Arthur; "our flat is OK, but yours is on fire".

---

* An elderly neighbour we knew in Salisbury used to do this test on their dining room table for her father who was a GP, when she was a young girl.

I have a distinct memory of the war in 1944 as a small child. My father thought the worst of the bombing was over and suggested we leave my grandparents where we had been staying, and come back to London. During this time there was a big raid in our area that destroyed a number of houses and killed people in Kenyon Street. My recollection is of me sitting on my mother's knee, under the stairs. Like many children then, I could not bear the sound of anything like an air raid siren, like my mother's vacuum cleaner, until I was about 15. I remember subsequently, finding a postcard to my parents which said; "I am taking my phenobarbitone", presumably administered because I couldn't sleep. Even after the war on many nights I lay awake because I was afraid my parents were going to leave me. I cannot imagine how awful it must have been, and still is, for the millions of children undergoing even longer periods of conflict. In the film "Hope and Glory" the star actor was a young boy who comes from a middle-class home by the Thames not far from London. Although his middle-class life was very different to mine, the film somehow evoked the atmosphere of the times.

Betty, my only female cousin told me of a visit with her parents to us in Fulham during the war. As she was a bit older than me, they took her up to London to see the sights. This included seeing the bomb-damaged houses with wall paper and curtains hanging out of windows, piles of rubble, bricks and wood and she thought it was "very pretty". Uncle Herbert was a very gentle fellow and his wife Flo was very loving*, but they were not amused and got cross with her and told her it was a naughty thing to say and she got a good telling off. A friend of ours out at a party at the end of the war said "I don't want the war to end", because it was all she had ever known. Betty also got into trouble when she approached my pram and was

---

* Flo used to give me a big kiss when I saw her, which I always tried to avoid.

told "not to go near the pram ever again". I can only think it was because my mother was worried about tuberculosis or some other infection before antibiotics came into use. Betty must have been a bit taken aback as she was always a bit afraid of my mother from then on. She eventually married Henry, also a miner, and she had a strong character as she refused to take money or gifts from one of the journalists who tried to use her as a source of information for the miner's strikes in the 60's.

Herbert and Flo's house in Whitwick near Swannington had an outside toilet at the bottom of the garden equipped with newspaper for toilet roll. When they finally left the house the cracks in the walls were wide enough to see the buses going past, due to the mining over many years causing subsidence.

I was baptised in St. Peter's church, Walton-on-the-Hill, which had one of the last Norman fonts left in England and where we sometimes stayed with friends in the holidays. In the autumn, we collected hazelnuts and chestnuts from the surrounding woods; those chestnuts roasted on an open fire were the best I can ever remember. In the Spring, it was common to see cyclists going back to London with large bunches of bluebells strapped to their bikes, apparently giving little thought to the damage they were doing to our wildflower population.

On occasion we stayed with another of my mother's cousins, Doris, married to Bill, who joined the RAF during the war but returned to be a butler on a large estate owned by shipping magnates, Lord and Lady Roydon. Thinking we were well away from bombs and deep in the Hampshire countryside and far from any town, one night we were surprised by some very loud explosions; later it was assumed it was a German bomber unloading its weapons. I remember seeing the craters afterwards in the countryside nearby.

My grandparents, lived in Swannington, a village in Leicester-shire. Everybody who could, kept pigs fed on food scraps and anything else they could get hold of. Even now, I can recall hearing the noise of the pigs squealing when they were taken to be slaughtered, it was as though they knew their fate. Some pigs were dealt with in the back yard, and black pudding made from buckets of blood made into a sausage, became one of my favourite foods.

My grandfather kept chickens at the bottom of his garden and I was once seen chasing them around the chicken coop shouting "I'll make the buggers lay!" I probably picked up that, and a few similar phrases from Edgar the village blacksmith and distant cousin. A visit to the smithy was a favourite passtime; the sound of the hammer on the anvil could be heard in the village below. My grandfather took me to see him when he was still making shoes for the shire horses, fitting them to the horse's hoofs in a cloud of smoke – from whence came the usual bad language. Years later in metal work class when making a poker for our coal fire, I discovered how heavy the tools were when working on an anvil. Taking the white-hot poker out of the forge, hammering it into the right shape while it was hot, then plunging it into water with a great cloud of steam was great fun. I also made a spoon out of copper. When I showed the master, I wanted to make the handle in the shape of a Maltese cross, he said it couldn't be done, but I managed it with some determination.

My grandfather could hardly read or write* and would not go to his daughters' weddings if they got married outside of Leicestershire as he did not want "to leave England". If he didn't like what was on television, he would say "turn it off, it's a waste of petrol". He also took me gleaning, which was gathering corn left over after the harvest, that we gave to the chickens. When church members used to come collecting for the village church, he would say he was 'Chapel' and when they were collecting for Chapel, he's said he was 'Church',

---

* although he managed to learn the names of horses for putting a bet on!

but he never went to either of them. In the 1930's miners' strike, he was listed as a 'pauper' but he refused to take the money from the union and said "no-one's gonna call me a bloody pauper!" Although he wouldn't take the extra money, they must have needed it because my aunts said that they had to share shoes and clothes with their sisters as they couldn't afford new ones.

My grandmother, Helen, could just about read – she would go to her children's weddings and even went on holiday with her sisters to Blackpool. She made lemonade by putting a piece of yeast on a small piece of toast in a bottle of water with some lemon juice and sugar, kept it for a week and would then sell it to the local children for a penny a bottle. Like other families, she also made elderberry wine. Her brother-in-law, Tom, was married to Aunt Luce. The story goes that they had two little girls and when they got home from school, they said to their mother that "daddy was lying in a ditch". Aunt Luce said "the bugger can stay there for all I care". When Arthur took Doris (his new wife), to see Aunt Luce she looked at her and said "So you're the London gal?". But Doris could stand up for herself and said "Yes, that's me". They said that my mother, Lucy, was named after Luce and she must have been a bit like her because they said she was "Luce b' name and Luce b' nature", which explains why I was always a bit afraid of her – not to mention the rest of the family!

My grandparents had 10 children, of whom only one died aged 15 from tuberculosis. One other, Florrie, lived into adulthood, but was permanently ill with heart problems but she often helped to look after me when we went to stay. Sometimes, she would take me and a little girl who lived a few doors away to the surrounding fields for a picnic: where the ancient remains of agricultural work could be seen as furrows. There was a derelict windmill that we used to visit which I am pleased to say has now been restored. We picked blackberries in the autumn and rosehips, which If I didn't eat my dinner my grandfather would say "Gi 'im so peckhaws" – they weren't very pleasant!

At Swannington station it was said that a railway accident here persuaded the authorities to fit steam whistles on the engines. This piece of technology allegedly spread throughout the world from this one small village in 1833. We would travel from London to Leicester by the London, Midland and Scottish railway (LMS), then change for Coalville and sometimes again for Swannington and usually would arrive quite late at night. You could lower the window of the old carriages, stick your head out and get soot in your eyes, which as a small boy was considered 'fun'. When we arrived, there was always a meal of eggs, bacon and black pudding waiting for us. I vividly remember getting out onto the platform while the engine hissed and a porter would collect our baggage*. On the return journey going back to London, I would look out of the window as we left the countryside behind and got into the suburbs with all the buildings seemingly crowding in on us, the tears were running down my cheeks. I expect my mother felt the same way.

Like his brothers, uncle Arthur was called up during the war and was stationed in Malta at a vital period, as an anti-aircraft gunner, when one gun in four was to remain silent, even during an air raid, due to a shortage of ammunition. However, they still trained their guns on the enemy and he realised they had a German plane in their sights, so he ordered his mates to fire. Two out of four shells hit the plane which was destroyed. We don't know whether he was put on a charge or not for disobeying orders.

Incidentally, his wife Doris also had a close shave with the enemy. She was walking along Woodlawn Road in Fulham when

---

* Many of these country stations have all been closed as described in the song by Flanders and Swan – 'The Slow Train'

the milkman ahead of her shouted at her to 'get down!' as a German fighter was firing at pedestrians. That evening on the BBC news it was reported that a German plane had been strafing people in Fulham. "That's me!" she said with great pride. She was so pleased with herself; you'd think she was keeping up with her husband's notoriety!

Street life

"One would be in less danger, from the wiles of a stranger,
*if one's own kin and kith, were more fun to be with"**

Uncle Jo was the eldest, and in civilian life he was in charge of a shunting engine, pushing coal trucks in and out of sidings. In war time, when he was stationed in Europe, he was put in charge of a long-range gun which ran on rails with a 20-mile range. He came home with a large German knife in a scabbard engraved with the name Wilhelm on the blade, which he gave to me. I remember roaming the streets of Fulham as a youngster with the knife on my belt which gave me a sense of security as I was always targeted by local lads. When writing this chapter, a hidden memory came back to me, where a boy who I thought was a friend, tried to drag me into an alley way, and would have assaulted me. I know I fought and screamed to get away and never went near their house again and avoided their street, but I never told my parents. On another afternoon I was leaning against a lamppost looking down Woodlawn Road, and I could see the barrage balloon at Wormwood Scrubs, and sometimes you could see people leaping out of it, presumably doing parachute training. While I was looking at this, a bunch of kids

---

* Ogden Nash, *Family Court*, 1931.

passed by me and one of them punched me in the face, hitting my head on the lamppost. Sometimes I also had to run away from kids in Swannington, but I could get away more quickly as I could hear them coming – although I preferred being in the country, I wasn't any safer! Although things weren't as bad as they are now with the gangs and the knife crime there is today, somehow, we accepted a certain amount of mild violence – it seemed only natural, but once I got to grammar school and had homework, my life on the streets came to an end.*

My uncle Ernest operated a dummy searchlight to detract the German bombers in Hampshire. He and Arthur used to argue furiously about religion. Herbert didn't get called up and stayed down the mines. Ron, the youngest son, was stationed in North Africa as a cook. If any family came to stay, we would all muck in and sleep in the same beds. Ron (the family comedian), would describe to me how he saw planes crashing down in the desert. I remember riding pillion with him on his motorbike, until after one night in Fulham, I saw a motorbike whizz round a bus and

---

* When I came back from Nigeria before I started work on malaria I got involved with some young volunteers as part of a charity, who were redecorating a house for chaps who had just come out of Wandsworth prison. Two of the inmates who were due to be released at some time were going to join us to do the work. I was asked to pick them up from Wandsworth prison in the Ford Anglia which I did, and got to know them a little bit. One of them was a Canadian who had been in prison for much of his life. I asked him how did his criminal life begin he said that he had stolen some apples or something like that and was due to be up before a magistrate. His mother said to him, if they ask you do you want to go away say yes, which of course he did. From then on, he spent his life in and out of jail. He said one of the problems when you are out of jail is that the only friends that you have are from the criminal fraternity. It seemed to me not only was it a sad story but how easily people can slip into the wrong path. I thought how things could have gone wrong for me wandering around the streets of Fulham with a knife in my belt.

knock over an old lady. I didn't go on the bike with him again after seeing that.

One cousin operated the cage that took miners up and down the mineshaft. At the end of his shift when his replacement turned up drunk, he said he would stay on to work the man's shift. The foreman asked why he didn't want to go home for a meal, to which he replied "not worth it, it's only a 100 to 1". When the foreman asked what he meant, he said, "there was only 100 to 1 chance there'd be any meat" in his supper.

On one of our visits, Henry, Betty's husband, said of his mates: you would never show any weakness; "if a pile of rocks fell on you, you didn't dare cry for help". The men would say "you alright Henry? We're just goin' for 'uz snap (lunch)". But they would dig him out eventually! One miner was hit in the face by a bolt from a drill, and it took three quarters of an hour through a tunnel that was two and a half feet high, to get him first aid. Just another example of why mining was a dangerous occupation, which in some men generated a harsh attitude to life. Uncle Ted used to charge his wife, Irene, for vegetables from his allotment. His standard phrase was "what I've found in life is…". After he died she said she'd always hated him but divorce was never considered. She didn't trust the government or banks, so after Ted died, she kept her savings in £10 notes under the carpet!

As a youngster, at the bottom of our street (Kenyon Street), were the wharves on the Thames. I used to lie in bed and listen to the sirens and the hooting of the tug boats on a foggy night, as they towed 'lighters' (barges), up and down towards the London docks. In those days everybody had coal fires and especially in November, you would get 'smog': very thick fog that caused the death of thousands of people from the deadly mixture of smoke from coal fires and the gases they produced.*

---

* After this time coal fires were banned and smokeless fuel was brought in.

On one particularly cold winter, there was a heavy fall of snow and the trolley buses would block the main roads, which meant more traffic than usual down our road. I saw a lorry near our front door unable to get going, so I got the front door mat and threw it under the back wheel and off he went with a cheery wave. I also remember a night watchman's hut, which had a brazier in it, that was lovely and warm and cosy. I think he was supposed to be guarding the building materials for the bomb-damaged houses. Apart from bomb sites, we played football in the road, as there were few cars. But as usual I was the last person picked for any team because I was too skinny. At school, when they started a team, I had to have a play-off with one of the boys to see who would be in it – he was about twice my size, so you can guess who got in.

We were always being shouted at by old ladies worrying about their windows, but if we went to Bishop's Park, the park keepers used to shout at us there too. On rare occasions we could earn a sixpence by helping the milkman collect the empty bottles. Other

Finlay St football team; Geoff is 3rd on left back – before being kicked off

ways of passing the time included rolling coloured glass marbles along the gutters to knock one marble out of the way (there were no dogs around, to mess the pavements). We also swapped cigarette cards that had badges of RAF squadrons, naval ships or army regiments on them that you could win from other players. We also played the ancient game of 'five stones' – throwing one in the air to catch while picking another up. Climbing up the street lamps was another activity, which we also got in trouble for. We must have played cowboys and Indians inspired by Saturday morning pictures at the cinema. The films were always in black and white with the Lone Ranger and Tonto. On the radio, there was the Dick Barton special agent at a quarter to seven in the evening and PC49, the story of a London copper. The *Eagle* comic came out monthly when I was around 10 or 11 and that was something I bought every now and then. This told the adventures of Dan Dare and Digby in their spaceship Anastasia versus the Mekon, alongside the stories based on the Walls Ice Cream boy and the travels of St Paul that were also included. The middle spread opened out to show a diagram of the inside of a steam engine, aeroplane, car or boat, to explain the workings of the machinery, which I found fascinating. If the *Eagle* was still published, no doubt the spread would be all about computers and technology.

Back then, Sundays were very different as after church and Sunday School we would sometimes walk to Bishop's Park, but I wasn't allowed to jump around or play with a ball. The only attraction at Bishop's Park was an ice cream seller called Mrs Santilli, selling her ice cream from a wooden cart. Over the years she progressed from a small handcart, to a bigger cart, an electric powered cart and then eventually to a van. The ice-cream was delicious – a penny a cornet.

In 1947, a friend of my fathers offered him the opportunity to buy a house in Cloncurry Street, close to Bishop's Park for £1000. It needed £100 spending on it, but as my father would have had to get a mortgage, on his wages he didn't think he'd be able to afford it. I think some of the properties there are now going for about 2.5 million – gosh, wouldn't life have been different if he'd taken the plunge!

During the 1950's there was what was called an 'export drive' to sell as many cars and other vehicles, especially fire engines, to foreign countries and these were all parked during the day in the streets near us, presumably waiting to be transported from the wharves. During the night, they often took out the batteries to keep them safe. The first car we bought was an old Ford which had been sitting in a field in Hampshire with the doors open and chickens popping in an out of it. I learnt to take the battery out and learned a little about the engine. Its top speed was 50 miles an hour, but it only had two springs and used to wobble if you went that fast. It had vacuum operated windscreen wipers, which slowed down when you accelerated. To save the battery, it was often started by a handle, until one day the handle reversed and broke my father's wrist, so it was sold. They didn't get another car until their retirement in the 1970's, probably because they couldn't afford to support me at college along with the upkeep of the car.*

I think my mother must have been very lonely when I was a child, as she had no family near, except for Arthur and Doris who had no children and would work during the week. She had been very attached to her family and it was a long time before she began to know other mothers at the Congregational church. At week-ends my father still worked at the United Dairies and we would to go to the 'rag shops' by bus to Putney, but without buying very much. Once we went to Arding and Hobbs in Clapham for school uniform. The buses had conductors who would punch a hole in your one and a

---

* I contributed when I could, doing odd jobs during holidays.

half pence ticket.* On rare occasions, we went to Roehampton when it was still a village before the tower blocks arrived and it was like being in a village in the country. A memorable occasion was going to Bentals in Kingston, where I had my first meringue.

For a while, my mother worked part-time as a cleaner for the Greens (related to Graham Green the author), in Kensington and she used to do our shopping in the North End Road carrying it all on the number 74 bus on the way home. When I got older, I used to get quite a bit of shopping, carrying it on my bike handlebars. Later on, when I was at college on the odd occasion I met a friend, we would cycle to Richmond Park and read poetry or just lie back and listen to the skylarks.

One particular summer Mr Green, who was a coffee merchant, took his wife for a prolonged holiday to Brazil. They needed someone to look after the house in South Kensington so we stayed there for the whole summer. I had a small bike so I used to cycle around South Kensington and had a great time sailing my small yacht on the round pond in Kensington Gardens.

Later, although no longer a cleaner, my mother was asked by the Greens to cook for them on special occasions, one of which was for the Portuguese ambassador. After the meal he went especially into the kitchen to congratulate her on her culinary skills. She got the job through another cousin Ethel Gates, when she started with Mrs Green in Battersea, and then, when they moved to South Kensington they used to each work on alternate days. When I came back from Nigeria, Mr Green and his new wife, very kindly invited me to dinner as they had asked about my time there, so I spent an evening showing them my photographic slides. Mr Green was so

---

* This was before Routemaster buses and were RTW, RMW Rolls Type buses, the kind you see on old films with Michael Cain.

different from other English businessmen whom I had experienced briefly in Nigeria, as he had a warm and friendly manner.

Ethel Gates lived in a small terraced house off York Road in Battersea which, when I was a child, had trams running through it. Ethel had two children but her husband became very violent, possibly due to falling off a lorry and damaging his head. I only saw him once as he was in one of the mental hospitals in Banstead.* I can only remember a lorry parked in a big open space from which a lot of men in blue uniforms were brought to meet their families. Ethel was a remarkable lady who was never without a smile and a giggle despite having very little money. There was always some problem with her house, such as a leaking roof that the landlord simply ignored. The road was a cul-de-sac, so all the neighbours knew each-other and supported each-other through thick and thin. After the war all of those small terrace houses were demolished and replaced by tower blocks. She was then moved to the 14th floor of a tower block and given a new washing machine and was by all accounts very happy there. By then her children had left home, but my parents stayed there one night and said they didn't sleep because of the noise from the freight trains below and the helicopters above, from the base down the road.

In contrast, later, once I was married, another lady we knew was moved to the ground floor of another tower block in Battersea, which made her vulnerable to the local kids banging on the door and being a general nuisance. Somehow we were involved in visiting her, possibly through church connections as they wanted to invite her to a Christmas party. Most of the time she was in a terrible state because one of her daughters was a high-class prostitute who used

---

* Near Horton Hospital, where they used a malaria treatment for syphilis (see later).

to bring expensive toys for the nieces, although the mother did not want them. The main reason for her fear was that there had been a spate of murders of prostitutes and she was terrified this was going to happen to her daughter. She lived on sleeping pills and whisky. When I went to collect her for the Christmas party I was a bit late picking her up and she was so afraid I wasn't going to come, she had consumed quite a lot of whisky. However, she stayed awake all through the party and consumed everything that was edible in sight, sweeping the crumbs in to her handbag before we left – it was amazing was how she managed to stay awake at the party after all she had consumed. She was an example of someone who was moved into an estate which really didn't suit her because she was taken away from her old neighbours from whom she would have had support. We felt sad for her, but helpless to change her situation.

Hopeless holidays

When the war finished and I was quite young, our summer holidays were invariably taken at seaside resorts, such as Llandudno, Isle of White and Skegness. My father wanted us to go with the Workers Educational Association as a group, but my mother wouldn't go on anything like that, I think due to her shyness. I remember one embarrassing occasion when my mother said that the potatoes in the boarding house where we were staying, smelt of TCP and it caused considerable embarrassment – I wanted to hide under the table. As we couldn't stay in the boarding houses during the day, if the weather was inclement, which it invariably was, we spent a lot of time sheltering in bus shelters to keep warm or a café if we were allowed to spend some money. Everywhere seemed to be brown and wherever we went I remember swirls of cigarette ends like confetti, collecting in corners on the street. The light relief was meeting up with my aunts and uncles Betty and Ron, Kit, Edmund and Florrie, as there were no other children around. When we stayed in South Kensington, I used to go to the geological museum to look at their collections. Whilst on holiday, one thing I did to amuse myself was to create my own museum of a collection of things I found, such as stones, rocks and shells and put them in a box with cotton wool. Ron and Betty were quite impressed by this. Recently I read an article by Germane Greer in which she described how her parents dragged her off to the beach every weekend which was the traditional Australian pastime and she longed to do something more interesting. She described her childhood as lonely and boring and when I think of my childhood and teenage years it sometimes sounds very similar.

We must have gone to Sandgate in Kent at one stage, where my great grandfather on my father's side lived after retiring from the army where he served in the Royal Artillery. According to my father, he started life as a plough boy in Suffolk and later ran away to join the army at 14. He built up a rapport with the Canadian troops in the Shorncliffe camp nearby. When he died in 1916 they gave him a military funeral on a gun carriage as he'd fought in the Crimea and the Indian Mutiny. On the anniversary of his battles, he would raise a flag on the flag pole outside in his garden, so he must have been a character. His son, my grandfather was an expert rifle shot who won many medals which he kept in a glass case. I didn't know him, as he died when I was young and my mother fell out with my grandmother for reasons unknown. We never saw her even though she lived locally to us but my father would visit on his own.

On one 'holiday by the sea' I have a highly embarrassing photograph of me in a swimming costume knitted for me by my mother – let's just say, wool is not the best material for swimming costumes. I don't think it helped my enjoyment of the seaside. She

Great grandfather George Butcher, wearing his Crimea and Indian Mutiny medals

liked to save money by making my clothes, but she never got it quite right. I was not allowed a belt and had to have braces to hold up my short trousers but these didn't fit and the braces allowed my trousers to bounce up and down as I walked along. I fished for crabs on the beach, but never managed to catch any. The highlight of the holiday was because it was the year in which we invaded Egypt with the French, so at Shorncliffe camp all the army vehicles were painted in desert colours. I remember seeing someone operating a flame thrower, which was a truly terrifying weapon.

I only met him once, but my father had a brother, who was about 10 years younger, (Don Butcher, son Peter) who was an expert in squash. He wrote a book which became a standard 'textbook' for the sport, and was highly regarded. During the war he was in the RAF as ground staff and later emigrated to Australia.

Primary school

My first school was Finlay Street Primary school run by the LCC (London County Council), where I started aged 5. It had classrooms lit by gas, with filaments that were forever breaking, generating great excitement.

During and after the war, I think there was a shortage of teachers, but some of them I can remember very clearly. There was a Mr Peters, who was a middle-aged chap who I remember particularly because he was so patient and taught us basic subjects such as English and maths. He was unusually kind, and almost treated us as adults. In contrast, there was a Miss Buckle of whom we were all scared, dressed entirely in black with a neat black hairnet and bright red lipstick. My desk was right at the front and one afternoon, she looked at me and said, "are you alright Geoffrey?" to which I replied that I had a headache. I was given a special treat of a sugar cube, although this kind gesture didn't stop me feeling afraid of her. Another teacher, Mr Algy, had been a prisoner of war in Germany and he would read stories to us, during which, one little boy in the class called Colin, was forever making a nuisance of himself. One way or another, Colin didn't pull any punches and told the teaches exactly what he thought of them. One afternoon Mr Algy was so frustrated, he picked Colin up by the seat of his trousers and smacked his bottom – you could see a cloud of dust appearing from his trousers. There was another who had been a Sargent in the Irish Republican Army and he taught us how to draw Roundheads and Cavaliers – I used to spend my evenings attempting to draw them. Perhaps this is why I have always found the history of the civil war especially interesting.

Our Headteacher was a Mrs Davidson, whose grey hair was fixed tightly back in a bun. When she took assembly, she had her hands clenched in front of her and eyes shut tight as she led us in singing hymns. She could be very strict; I remember being told off for sitting on a table when I should have been sitting on a chair. One day, I sat down and the chair was taken away by the boy behind whereupon I banged my head, which must have produced lots of blood which they bandaged up, which made me feel rather special. Mrs Davidson lived next door to my uncle Arthur and aunt Doris in Epsom and she would keep them informed about my progress. But she showed no predilection for things microscopical although it was probably Mrs Davidson who advised my parents that I should go to Emanuel when I passed the 11 plus. I can remember, on the morning of the exam, some of us were dosed up by our mothers who produced a brown bottle of Radio Malt, a mixture of glucose and vitamins, to help us get through the ordeal.

On the first morning of going to Emanuel, getting on the trolley bus with other boys from that area, all of us were scared. As we got on board, one anxious mother called out to us to look after her son

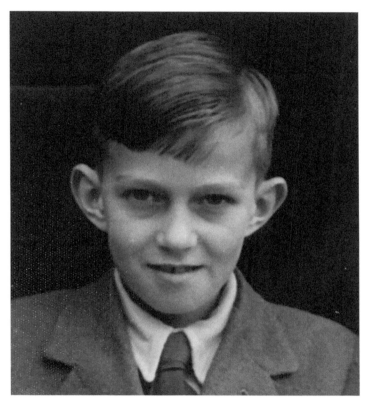

Geoff age 11

but we were more concerned with looking after ourselves! We had to wear the school uniform; a black jacket with a portcullis badge, plus tie and cap. We were supposed to buy the jacket from Harrods, which was not only expensive, but was discovered to have moths. I remember my mother was very cross, took it back and bought one from a less expensive shop, eventually sewing on the badge at a later date; another reason which left me feeling out of place.

Emanuel Grammar School: rebellious beginnings

My generation was one of the first to sit the 11 plus exam and through passing this, enabled me to go to Emanuel School in Battersea. This was a direct grant school, founded in 1594 by Lady Acre, a friend of Queen Elizabeth I. Like many other working-class children who got through the exam, I found myself in the unfamiliar environment of a middle-class grammar school. Not knowing where I was supposed to be, and what to do next for reasons I cannot remember, I found myself up before the Deputy Head, Captain W.S. Hipkins, (he was nicknamed 'Pump' as his initials W.S.H. stood for 'water supply here'). As I stood trembling in my boots, he said to me "Where do you come from boy?" I said "Fulham sir". To which he replied "Oh that's not a very good area, is it?". Perhaps it's not surprising that I did not feel entirely welcome. As far as I can remember, the only positive comment I received that gave me some encouragement in all the time I was at Emanuel, was from the chemistry master who said "You're a good chemist Butcher, but you waffle."

In A level, we handled all sorts of chemicals, including mercury that you wouldn't be allowed to use now, and used to bubble hydrogen sulphide gas through various solutions. When I was at home with my chemistry set, I used to take old batteries apart and do various experiments of my own making. I was careful about acids, but I did manage to fill my mother's kitchen with chlorine one afternoon – I had to open all the doors and windows in our small flat to get rid of the odour – possibly the beginning of losing my sense of smell!

It was only the fascination of science subjects that kept me going along with history, geography and metal work. The thing I hated most was sport because of my size – rugby was torture and cricket was unadulterated boredom, even though for some people it may represent some kind of good middle-class behaviour; "play up and play the game". Many boys from my background left school long before completing their education. I didn't realise it at the time, but I was a typical "Marsden and Jackson" case* in which they reported on the fate of working-class children who had been to grammar school and found themselves, as I had done, in a completely foreign environment. It was a difficult struggle; both to do the studies and mix with fellow students. The stress was compounded in many cases, including myself, because we also felt totally out of place at home and our parents ceased to have anything in common with us. A particular example, one afternoon when I got home after school, I said to my mother: "I had a smashing physics lesson today"; all she replied was "straighten your tie." My father put it bluntly when I overheard him saying to someone: "We lost Geoffrey when he went to grammar school". He only went to one parents' evening and wouldn't go again because the skin on his hands was so rough from handling milk crates.

These problems didn't arise in every school. Some pupils who were especially clever and/or good at sports, seemed to sail through the whole experience without a care in the world. Others formed themselves into groups for mutual support, while others went to schools of the same type but at least adapted their procedures

---

* "Education and the Working Classes" Brian Jackson and Dennis Marsden

and curriculum to the needs of the boys, instead of the other way around. So, for example if the boys wanted to play football instead of the usual public-school rugby, they were allowed to play football. One friend of mine was very keen on squash, but as it wasn't played in the school, one of the masters took him on his motorbike to other schools every weekend to play. A girl from our neighbourhood in Fulham who had a scholarship to a boarding school, went to see the headmistress when she was in the sixth form and had a similar experience to mine. The headmistress said to her "we really don't like having people like you at this school, we'd rather you went away". Perhaps this was because her father was a gas man.

I had one more "interview" with Captain Hipkins at about the time I was supposed to join the Cadet Force (age 14). He said: "you haven't joined the cadet force Butcher!?"

"No, sir"

"You're a feeble cabbage, Butcher! What are you?"

"A feeble cabbage, sir"

And so ended my military career. I could see no good reason to spend an afternoon being shouted at by some power-mad prefect, wearing a uniform that was certainly too big for me, boots likewise, when I could be at home getting on with my homework and getting what I thought was a useful education. As National Service had ceased I felt secure in my conviction. When they had their yearly inspection, the staff who had been in the World Wars would turn up, some of them, in their first world war uniform, one of whom was the Latin master. Though I couldn't stand Latin, he was such a nice man and he had a long row of medals, I almost felt guilty for not joining up.

It may be some indication of how some pupils thought about the school when I was there, because there were four attempts to set fire to it, which a fireman told me was not that uncommon at the time. The last major effort succeeded in burning down the physics lab and

I nearly lost my notes, but the final attempt was only a smouldering pile of papers at the door of the geography room. If you look at the website for Emanuel school now, pastoral work is very prominent and it is clear that the school is a much happier and successful place to be, with notable old boys, one of whom is Tim Berners Lee.

My one relief from the pressures of school and home was having the independence that comes from cycling. I would go on trips to Richmond Park or further afield to Heathrow to watch the planes, when it was still a collection of huts. At first the planes were all propeller powered, such as the Bristol Britannia but eventually jet engines became the norm, the first being the Comet. I once went, with a few other boys, cycling to Whitstable – about 52 miles to the coast. On the way back, I got lost in London, but managed to find my way home by following the river. Cycling throughout my life has been my one regular activity and I would always cycle to work, wherever possible.*

Although I worked hard at my A Levels in physics, chemistry, botany and zoology (including two extra papers on zoology and chemistry plus the practical exams), I was surprised to learn that I had been awarded a state scholarship, which should have given me great opportunities to go to an appropriate university†. I knew I

---

* I managed to carry on cycling until my late 70's when Parkinson's finally made me give up my fold up bike.

† In those days, Oxford and Cambridge set their own exams and one of the questions was "if you were a dog in a sputnik (Russian satellite), where would you like to land? The choices were the Vatican, the Pentagon or the Dean of Canterbury's garden. Discuss. Answer: If you landed in the Vatican you'd probably be ignored as the Italians didn't care much for dogs at the end of the war. If you landed in the Pentagon as a Russian, they were bound to dissect you. If you landed in the Dean's garden, not only are the English mad about dogs but the Dean had allegedly, Communist sympathies so that's where you landed. This is the kind of question that would be discussed in middle class lounges, but not in working class kitchens.

wouldn't survive Oxford or Cambridge and I didn't get any advice from anyone on courses or subjects, so somehow I drifted into a zoology and botany course at Kings College London, although I had other offers from other universities. I think I would have liked to do biochemistry or microbiology once I'd started, but I wasn't aware of the courses or that one could change. Three years later, at the end of my time at Kings, the Head of Department (Professor J Danielli FRS) told me that if I had gone to him at the time, he would have found some appropriate course for me at another college. Another instance of my ignorance of how things worked. Although I got the state scholarship, I didn't think that this was anything special. In my mind I put it down to the fact that I'd worked very hard and this was not down to intellectual ability. I had the same feelings later about being offered a PhD post by Professor Danielli when he was moving to Buffalo in the USA. This could be down to my mother's Methodist background, which said you "don't push yourself forwards" and I was always cautioned "not to be boastful". I could never understand how some people could say they wanted and expected to became a professor or obtain some other senior position by the time they were forty. I didn't ever understand from where they got their confidence for such ambition.*

---

* I am equally perplexed by the excessive jollifications when today's youngsters discover they have passed their exams. To my generation, you got on with what you were expected to do without a fuss. A certain amount of celebration is acceptable by close family, but all this hysteria shown on the TV, seems odd to me. I think my parents went the other way in not particularly celebrating anything; although I would have celebrated having a bike for my birthday.

Zoology at Kings College London.

Kings College London was an Anglican Foundation to counteract the secular influence of University College London (So called "the Godless institution of Gower St"). As the Duke of Wellington, one of the founders of KCL remarked: "educate a man without religion and you make him but a clever devil". Perhaps he was right in his thinking that if you have technology and knowledge without humanity, you can get into trouble. As part of the first two years on the first Monday of each term there were lectures on theology and philosophy, followed by an exam. If you passed (and everybody did) then you were entitled to put AKC after your name – Associate of Kings College (which nobody did). I particularly remember the lectures by HD Lewis, a little Welshman. His lectures were on linguistic analysis which I found fascinating at the time, but sadly cannot now remember what it was all about.

In the first two years of the degree course, I did botany and zoology. Much of the zoology course was devoted to evolution and looking at old fossils, which I found extremely boring – I much preferred experimental work. We must have done studies on and dissected real animals, most of which I have now forgotten. But one dissection I do remember, was a final exam where I had to dissect and expose the blood vessels around the heart of a snake and as you can imagine, these were confined in a very small cavity. Although the snake had been killed, it's heart was still beating and continued to beat despite having 70% alcohol poured over it several times throughout the exam, to try to stop it. Obviously this made dissection much more difficult. At the end of the exam, I went back to the lab and I saw the lecturer, looking at my excavation, with a look of disdain on his face – clearly not happy with my work, but thankfully I managed to pass. The only thing I remember in botany was being taught to draw sections of plants under the microscope, which was much more difficult than it sounds. The lecturer was a slave driver but at least we got through it and learnt a useful skill. Since then, in my spare time, I used to paint watercolours of native flowers wherever we moved to, which I enjoyed immensely.

An important part of the zoology departments research was concerned with genetics outside the cell nucleus and this work was done on *Amoeba proteus*, a one-celled free-living protozoan supposedly to be found in pond water, though I've never found any. I discovered that I could dissect these amoebae under the microscope, just using a very fine glass fibre. I could cut off a 'pseudopodium' – this was an extension of the amoeba rather like a foot – and then much to my surprise, the membrane sealed up and by dragging this "foot" it followed the fibre on the slide, until it ran out of energy. I demonstrated these tricks to impress the students* when I was teaching at Midsomer Norton Grammar School where I later did my teaching practice. Little did I know, fifty years later, I'd be doing the same sort of dissection under a microscope with mosquitoes for malaria vaccine trials.[†]

As part of the zoology course, we were required to do a research project. I discovered an article in the *Observer* newspaper in which

---

* When the university lecturer on my PGCE course came to assess my potential as a teacher in Midsomer Norton, I was somewhat anxious as the class I had was the last period on a Friday with a group of not very clever or enthusiastic 15 year olds. Remembering my fun with my ten-shilling microscope from Coalville, I obtained some rhubarb and persuaded my pupils to look at a slither under the microscope. Much to my relief they found this really interesting and I was congratulated by the tutor. Rhubarb has remained a favourite food ever since, in addition to being a good working man's pudding easily grown in the gardens of Swannington.

[†] It is interesting to note that amoebae are now used as models in cancer research.

a Swedish research team claimed to have discovered how memory is stored. They worked on flatworms that have the most primitive brain in the animal kingdom but are also carnivorous. They claimed to have trained the worms to respond to some stimulus that they remembered, but when they fed the trained worms, chopped up, to the control worms the controls picked up the memory trace. My supervisor, at that time a PhD student (later became an FRS), did not agree with how I wanted to train them, so unfortunately, I did it his way and did not get any useful results, although the theory was probably flawed in the first place. This lesson taught me that even Fellows of the Royal Society can get it wrong! We used to have endless discussions after I had written an essay on the purpose of science. I spent an hour and a half discussing this with him in a tutorial, at the end of which he almost came round to agreeing with my conclusions. At the next session, we started all over again, though thankfully not for another hour and a half!

Although I only achieved a lower second for my first degree, Prof. Danielli FRS (joint discoverer of the structure of the cell membrane), was moving to a university in Buffalo, New York State, and asked me to go with him to do a PhD there in cancer research. He was my tutor for the last part of my degree course, which was the best part of my whole degree. He was a very brilliant and charming man and I've never been able to understand why he thought I might be worth taking on as a PhD student. At first, I was enthusiastic but when I looked at the application for a visa to do a PhD in the USA, I quickly changed my mind (in summary, this was 50 pages that asked whether you were a congenital idiot, did you want to murder the president or were you a communist?). I also discovered that Buffalo was not a particularly handsome city and cancer research was not one of my top interests. So perhaps, rather foolishly from a career perspective, I decided not to go and chose to take a more relaxing route forward through doing a PGCE (Post Graduate Certificate in Education), in Bristol. The positive side of this decision was that I avoided the possibility of being called up for the American forces (part of the deal to get the visa for the USA) and the risk of getting chloroquine resistant malaria fighting the communists in Vietnam.

Bristol: a year of discovery

As a preliminary part of doing the course at Bristol, we were expected to go to a local school to observe the students. I went to a school in West Kensington where there was a primary school downstairs and a secondary school on the first floor. The first class I observed was a group of 15 year olds who'd come from a run-down local Catholic school that had closed. They were bolshy and apparently difficult to control. The teacher who was assigned to teach them English, gradually impressed upon them how difficult life can be if you were unable to read and write your name and address and fill in forms, for say, any government bureaucracy. He spent the whole period getting this message across and I watched as these boys became increasingly subdued. The teacher told me he would be doing this for at least another three periods until it sank in.

In the primary school,* I listened to the staff talking about some of the children they had to deal with. I remember three examples of the behavioural problems. In those days, we had London County Council pens with sharp nibs that you dipped into the ink well in the desk; while a boy was writing and getting on with his work, his

---

* By pure chance, my wife Sue, had been teaching in this primary school, but our paths hadn't crossed at that point. She had quite a lot to do as she had about 40 children with 13 different nationalities, some of whom didn't speak English. One little boy could only be persuaded to sit down if you gave him a lot of stars to stick onto something.

left hand was on the desk and the boy next to him, picked up a pen and stabbed his hand, pinning it to the desk. Another example, was a boy who was so difficult, they sent for the police who duly turned up with a dog, whereby instead of the dog controlling the lad, the lad attacked the dog. Finally, one morning when the teacher did the register, she wanted to know why one of the boys was missing; they said he was up before a magistrate. He had picked up one of the piles of evening newspapers that vans used to distribute on to the pavement. This young lad, with great initiative, decided to go off to sell them, so he was up before the judge for his misdemeanour.

I'm not sure why this experience didn't put me off teaching completely, but it was the only profession that I had had experience of, coming from a working-class background to which I thought I could put my degree to good use. It never occurred to me that there were other professions to consider such as the law, economics or medicine.*

An even greater benefit of the course at Bristol was being tutored by the Director of Sports for the university: a Mr Jack Williams, who was also totally disinterested in the theories of education, or Plato or anybody else, but had a profound interest in people. He told us about a student who had been sent to him by the university doctors as they were very concerned about this boy who was doing a degree in chemistry, was an only child of elderly parents and was clearly an isolated sort of person. Jack had tried to get him to play badminton, I think in the hope of putting him into contact with people, though I don't think he succeeded. However, I realised to some extent I was like this student. I went to see him and he was immensely helpful to me in thinking through my struggles at home, school and university. He helped me to realise that it was probably a good idea to join the

---

* I also thought that when it got round to getting a job, Nigeria couldn't be worse that the teaching experiences I'd already had!

human race, so when Paul, one of my few friends, said there was a job in Nigeria for a biology teacher, I thought this might be a "good thing" and applied for the post. Knowing nothing of Africa or Africans and never having been abroad before, off I went on a Nigerian Airways Boeing 707 on a wet day in August 1963, much to the distress of my mother. We landed at night in Lagos airport in what seemed to be a hot, humid and smelly oven.

Nigeria

**"Beware and take care of the Bight of Benin,
For 40 goes out but only one comes in"***

Lagos Anglican Grammar School, founded in 1859,† was the oldest
school in Nigeria. In theory the boys came from different regions
of Nigeria, but I think most were Yoruba from the western side of
Nigeria. A few came from the eastern Igbo and virtually none from
the Hausa speaking north. And so, it began, two very happy years
away from home.

On my first day as a professional teacher, I expected to see neat
rows of boys all as keen as mustard to learn about science from
this young Englishman. It wasn't quite like that as I was the only
member of staff to turn up in one classroom of a block of six. In
the class I was supposed to be in charge of, the boys were having
a whale of a time shouting at the tops of their voice, leaping from
desk to desk and taking absolutely no notice of me. I decided it
was either them or me – most of whom were bigger than I was – so
I resorted to a couple of feet of rubber tubing, from which I had
kindly removed the Bunsen burner. This was the way things were

---

* A sea shanty about the risk of malaria in the Bight of Benin.
† We followed the English school system with the syllabus and exams from
the UK set by Cambridge University.

The road through Bariga on the way to the school front gate

done – Mr Iwigo*, the deputy Head, used to keep discipline with a long stick, and a big grin. Aside from the stick, he was a lovely man who was always very positive.

The official language of the school was English, and boys heard speaking in their native tongue were fined 3 pence, though since very few of them ever paid the school fees when they were supposed to, the three pence was rarely collected. Most English expatriate teachers arrived with the support and introduction to culture and language by the Voluntary Service Organisation, but my contract was directly with the school, so I had to work it out as I went along.

One of the most difficult obstacles to understanding biology in that environment was the complete absence of any text books adapted to West African plants and animals. The only text book we had available was an English standard text with, for example, 'the life cycle of the large cabbage white butterfly' despite the absence of any cabbages or the associated butterflies. So, the boys learnt what they could, purely by memorising the text book. Although we taught in English, it seemed to me, that the boys process of thinking was still in their native language. At advanced GCSE a common question in biology exams is "compare and contrast, e.g. respiration in plants and animals". None of the boys could answer this properly. They would describe a list of characteristics in plants and then a list of characteristics in animals but for some reason could not complete the question. I realised the difficulty when I showed them two different boxes of the same size but otherwise made of different materials, different colours etc. Someone suggested that the problem was in the native language there is no equivalent to "compare and contrast".

---

* Nigerian names I mention as I remember spoken, but I can't find the original spelling, so here they are written phonetically.

I couldn't refrain from trying a few experiments when I was teaching. I noticed that the plants (beans) seemed to grow more rapidly the deeper they were in a glass tube filled with soil. I arranged a row of tubes containing different volumes of mercury in small phials over a bean in each tube. There did seem to be some decrease in the time it took for beans to reach the top of the tube with a heavier weight to push up. The second experiment was an attempt to demonstrate to the students the passage of a nerve impulse. My friend Peter Vaughan at another school (Igbobi School), had an oscilloscope (like a primitive TV) and we connected this to a nerve dissected from a frog's leg. Unfortunately, we could see no impulse on the oscilloscope but we could hear the scope picking up the pilots talking to the control tower at Lagos airport on the speaker. Perhaps the nerve was acting as an aerial! I hope it entertained passing frogs, but it wasn't what we'd intended...

Amongst the other difficulties was the high turnover of staff, not only the English staff but the frequent change from English to Indian staff with the difficulties that that presented – each teaching English with their own tone and accent. In addition, there was little in the way of equipment: the biology lab had 19 hammers and two microscopes. I managed to collect a few specimens of different species; the most interesting of which were electric catfish which gave quite a shock (which I discovered from the market holder, who grabbed my hand and plunged it into the bucket!). I was able to get some third years interested by looking through the microscope at some cells scraped off the insides of their own cheeks. Most people are fascinated by this, and they were no exception. I also started a Biology Club as some of the boys were quite interested. One of them kept three crocodiles in a petrol tin in the boarding house, but he seemed to know how to keep them alive.

One of the challenges to doing any practical work in the lab was the erratic nature of the water supply. We had a three-story building with a water tank at the top and a pump at the bottom. This would have worked perfectly if it wasn't for the fact that the switch was on the third floor and was a simple pulley system and the boys used to amuse themselves by pulling off the string. One usually discovered that there was no water supply first thing in the morning and although you could re-unite the string with the pully, no water came through until after 2 o'clock (because of air in the pipes). By which time we teachers had vacated to the Lagos airport hotel for a drink, a swim and hopefully a view of the air hostesses.

A highlight of the year was the annual speech day in which we sat for hours in our academic gowns listening to long speeches, mostly in Yoruba, while we gradually melted away. Sports Day was another event rendered all the more exciting by javelins and heavyweights being flung in all directions at the same time.

My particular contribution to school life was getting boys to engage in some sort of charitable work such as reading to the blind, or collecting second hand clothes to help an orphanage. When we had enough clothes to make a worthwhile sale, we hired a hall in Lagos. This proved so popular I had to station the biggest sixth form boys on the doors to let everyone in at the same time and to stop people fighting over the clothes. It was pretty chaotic but we raised some money and one of our customers was the wife of the British High Commissioner, who looked as though she was wearing second-hand clothes already – or perhaps the latest fashion, I'm in no position to judge.

The inhabitants of the blind home that we visited, seemed to be mostly middle-aged men with whom we often had interesting discussions. For example, one topic that came up for discussion was the number of children one should have. One elderly man said that if God had given him ten children, he would give him the wherewithal to look after those ten children, seemingly forgetting that his children were being supported by other people while he was in a home. Since we left Nigeria the population has expanded dramatically. The idea of contraception or any form of birth control did not appeal to most Nigerians, no doubt partly from fear of disease, but also a matter of status. One of our senior sixth form pupils Ejemowa, said "when I come to England, I will marry one of your sisters". He could not believe that I was an only child. He and three other sixth form boys were keen on helping with our charity work; I regret that we didn't manage to remain in contact, they were a credit to themselves and the school and great fun to be with and teach.

Years later, much to my surprise at a meeting of the Wellcome Foundation, I was introduced to a Nigerian by a colleague from Imperial College. I discovered that the Nigerian had been educated at the Lagos Anglican Grammar school at the time I was there, but he said he didn't remember me. After another lecture, he turned and said "I remember you, you taught me to draw a Bunsen burner!". I remember the class in which he was a first-year pupil because I was supposed to teach them general science and that included how a Bunsen burner worked. But the other reason for remembering them was that hardly any of them had anything to write with, such as pens and paper. Like the English teacher in West Kensington, that was the first obstacle in their education that I had to overcome. I am pleased to say we have been in touch and he is now a consultant paediatrician with a continuing interest in malaria research. He recently sent me a poem that inspired his reasons for going into paediatric medicine; a feeling that I share:

"His Name is Today"
"We are guilty of many errors and many faults,
But our worst crime is abandoning the children,
Neglecting the fountain of life.

Dr Olugbemiro Sodeinde

Many of the things we need can wait.

The child cannot.

Right now is the time his bones are being formed,

His blood is being made,

And his senses are being developed.

To him we cannot answer 'tomorrow',

His name is Today."

by Gabriela Mistral, Chilean, Nobel Laureate, Literature 1945, and addition 'The child cannot.', Paediatricians' Poet; Olugbemiro Sodeinde

The only contact we had with the UK High Commission was during the first general strike in what the newspapers called "Black Africa". One of the ex-pats phoned the High Commission to ask if it was true that the Royal Navy was waiting off the coast to take us all home, to which the High Commissioner replied, "just keep your bath full, that's all we're doing down here", which became a sort of motto. The worst problem we encountered was when an African threatened to break the windscreen on our VW Beetle but somebody quickly gave him a few shillings and he ran off, without any damage.

Driving

Unfortunately, I did not have time to get an English/International licence before I left the UK, so my first ever driving licence was within an area known as Western Nigeria with a carefully designed driving test. After sitting for several hours under a palm tree in the hot sun, I was the first and only person that morning to pass the written test which included answering questions about an omolenkie (a sort of cart). After lunch was the practical driving test which involved measuring the width of your car and placing two rows of oil barrels which you had to reverse between at 90°. You were not allowed to make any corrections, which was virtually impossible; the whole test was designed so that you would bribe the police officer. I then took a test on Lagos Island which was still typically British, with British supervisors, and passed without any problem – or having to bribe anybody.

Having passed the theory, and the practical element of the driving test with an Englishman, I naturally assumed it would only take a few minutes in the office to get the business done and I would have my first ever one-year driving licence. No so. A Nigerian gent with power over a skinny Englishman, was in a powerful position. He noticed that on the form I handed to him was a small mark from a sticky Biro. "This cannot be passed!" "Why not?" I say. He points out the sticky mark and says "this is an alteration; the form is not therefore legal. Her Majesty would not approve." Meanwhile, Englishman is getting hot under collar, especially as the collar is already hot because of the climate. I rack my brains trying to think

Driving the back road to school

of something, or somebody that will avoid having to pay this man 'dash'. The aforesaid official may be in need of support for possibly his three wives and thirteen children, but not from me. At this point I remember another true-born Englishman who stayed on in Nigeria after independence, a certain Major Allen. He happened to be on the board of the grammar school and had a reputation for playing Chopin on his piano every morning before breakfast so he must be the right guy! So, I mention his name, whereupon officialdom grabs my hand, says "you know major Allen? Have your licence!" and off I go, happy to be able to drive and to serve this great country.

An aside ... it's not what you know ...

Many years later back in England, I was working at Imperial College on mosquitoes and infecting them with human malaria for vaccine trials. Although our mosquitoes became infected when we fed them blood from our cultures the results were rather erratic. Sometimes we had high infection rates and other times rather low levels. In order to do the trials, we needed a reliable infection in terms of numbers of parasites in the mosquitoes and enough mosquitoes to do trials on twenty volunteers. On occasion we had to import mosquitoes from the Walter Reed Army Institute of Medical Research in Washington. We decided to go and visit their facilities to see if we could improve our system. I went with my technician and when we arrived at Washington airport I went through immigration without any problem. I realised my technician was being held up. After a while I thought I would go and see what the problem was, so I went up to the lady in charge. The problem seemed to be my technician's passport which she had never used before, and they seemed suspicious. I then explained to her that we were going to the Institute working on malaria and mosquitoes. She immediately shook my hand and said "my husband is an entomologist, welcome to America!" and off we went thinking "supposing he'd been a plumber"? We might have spent the next two weeks hanging around the airport – officialdom is much the same the world over.

Years later I remember this incident at a meeting on World Malaria Day, held in a trade union office off Tottenham Court Road. There were very few people at the meeting (surprise, surprise), but there was a large group of Nigerian business women recognisable by their jocular mood and colourful garments which were probably about fifteen feet long. The meeting was not terribly interesting until a single black lady sitting at the back stood up and said "what Africa needs is less corruption". That was the first time ever I had heard a black person admitting corruption was a problem, which it was at all levels of society. I suppose it took us a couple of hundred years to reduce corruption (or at least to a degree), in this country, so we shouldn't be in too much of a hurry to expect its demise elsewhere.

Back to driving ...

It was essential to have a car as the only form of public transport were small VW mini buses. They only carried about 12 people and associated chickens. Driving was an interesting experience as even on the main roads there was only tarmac on the middle strip, so the tyres on the left ran on the laterite, which wore through very quickly. The long-distance transport was in lorries which used to drive in the middle of the road, occupying the entire width of the tarmac. The driver would lean out of the cab to keep himself awake, trusting in the religious and biblical sayings plastered over the lorry which he hoped would keep him alive. Sadly, this didn't always work.

Daily life

Most expatriates employed one or more Africans to do cooking and washing around the home, but Paul and I decided it wasn't worth employing full time help so we took on a short little Igbo chap called Johnson to do our washing and the occasional odd job. Johnson was a delight – he had a great sense of humour and was honest as the day is long. One of the little toes on his feet was only connected by a very thin piece of tissue, which he duly chopped off as it may have been more dangerous on than off. His prize possession was a radio (in his terminology "ladio"), which was quite big and he carried it on his head, but it had to be supplied fairly often with new "blatterlies". He had two wives who operated a kind of shuttle service, one remained in the East, where he came from and the other came to Lagos. When she got pregnant, they swapped over. He also did odd jobs for an English family (the Arnolds). The only occasion that we were rather cross with him was when he bought half a goat from one of the so-called, gardeners, and he left the head in our fridge with the blood dripping on the butter. The other thing he did was to chop up the skin of the goat, and boil it in one of our saucepans which then retained a horrible smell and was soon thrown away. One night he narrowly missed death as a green mamba which was coiled up on a shelf in the kitchen, struck at him at head height but fortunately missed. By coincidence, a newspaper article mentioned two teenage English boys were seen wandering around a supermarket carrying two poisonous snakes, probably green mambas, in a sack. The management was not pleased.

Another hazard were the soldier ants. One evening I decided to go to bed early, went in to the bathroom and was confronted by two rows of large black ants, marching along the length of the bath. I kept out of their way until 1 o'clock in the morning when they'd all

What's for supper? Goat

gone. They would swiftly collect together to get rid of anything in the way on whatever journey they were making. Any animal unable to move out of their way, would be eaten alive in no time at all.

Amongst the more interesting people that we met was an American missionary, Don, there with his wife and four beautiful daughters who we would meet at the airport hotel swimming pool. He had a whole menagerie of animals on his plot, including a chimpanzee, birds and rodents of some sort, but his biggest collection was snakes, constrictors and venomous among them. On one occasion, the obvious question he had was to find out how far the venom would travel from a spitting cobra. So, he put on a pair of swimming goggles and prodded it with a long stick. I think it managed about 7 feet. He had a cupboard where the snakes lived, some with triangular heads – these were the Gaboon viper; these have the longest fangs and the most potent venom of all venomous snakes, but happily, they are rather sluggish and lazy and not many people get bitten by them.

Perhaps the most interesting specimen was an 8-foot python which was maintained on a diet of puppy dogs – one a fortnight. Don was a big strong man and he would hold the head in his hand while it curled around his arm. One day he was showing some visitors this snake and I was holding the tail end when suddenly, it produced a huge volume of urine, which I managed to direct away from me and the visitors. We went on several snake hunting expeditions at night wading through streams in the hope of catching the occasional specimen to add to the collection. On one occasion one of Don's assistants let out a loud high-pitched scream and we naturally thought he'd been bitten and altogether, as one man, leapt out of the stream onto the bank thinking the worst. In fact, he had caught a beautiful orange coloured harmless snake. It was probably just as well he didn't know what was going through the minds of the rest of us.

Arthur Arnold and I organised an expedition to the bush with the local lads to see if we could see monkeys in their natural habitat. This was rather disappointing as we could hear them chattering but could not see any. We were badly bitten by mosquitoes and the next day I went down with a high fever and terrible headache. A Nigerian Army doctor examined me and said he would treat me for cerebral malaria which, according to my parasitology book, was invariably fatal. However, it could not have been malaria as this takes about two weeks to develop after being bitten and he never took a blood sample to examine it for malaria parasites. This was my only experience with malaria in Africa and being bitten by a large number of mosquitoes.

One of the afternoons round the swimming pool Mike (one of our history teachers), thought he would demonstrate to the air hostesses his prowess at handling Don's chimpanzee. Unfortunately, the chimpanzee had his own ideas and Mike got a nasty bite, much to the amusement of the rest of us, including the hostesses. Mike also had some more bad luck when he took on an African lad, James, who developed filariasis and we could see the worm in his eye. We spent hours waiting for him to be treated in a local clinic and Mike generously paid for his treatment. Sometime later, James disappeared with all of Mike's clothes and much of his cash. On another occasion, a young English missionary, Richard, woke up in the night to find an African rolling up his carpet, probably with more valuables inside. He duly chased after him, eventually caught him, which attracted a crowd of Africans and there was great commotion and shouting. In his posh English accent, Richard said to us later that he wondered if "this the sort of thing a missionary priest is supposed to be doing…?"

People often ask what we foods we were able to obtain. The food most readily available were goats and on our 50 acre site these survived on some poor-quality grass and anything else they could eat, especially paper – including all the books in the library that had been sent out by the British Council. One of the English teachers whose job it was to supervise the library, had therefore very little to do. It was not uncommon when you asked a boy why he hadn't done his homework, the reply was "de goats ate my book". On speaking to one of my ex-students, he said that they used the same excuse to their parents when they were given their report cards to take home but didn't want them to find out their results!

The English food in the Supermarket in Lagos was rather expensive so we existed on a variety of local and some imported foods. Yam instead of potato and local bread made with palm wine, which was rather nice. I tried growing some tomatoes, but they grew so fast they never had time to form and remained a green fruit that didn't mature. I also tried growing peanuts and couldn't understand why I didn't get any. It was only sometime after I realised peanuts grew underground, but I hadn't dug them up to find out! I cooked quite a few meals of goat (roasted, fried, grilled, stewed, boiled), which was very tender but a rather strange smell. It was better with spices, once I had discovered them. My first experience of sweet potato was obtained from two young boys, who walked around selling these from large enamel bowls they carried on their heads. I bought some ready-cooked sweet potato from them and enjoyed the crunchy taste on the inside. This, I later discovered when I bought some uncooked sweet potato, were caterpillars. The boys used to eat termites, fried, in the termite season, when the males started to fly about. There is little doubt with the world expansion of human populations that one day, eating insects will not be unusual.*

---

* In the West the idea only goes back to Victorian times and I have a recipe for sawflies and gooseberry and cream.

Farmer Geoff

The sweet potato seller

Kano

During my time in Nigeria we went on a few expeditions and visited Kano, the biggest and probably oldest city in the North and the capital of the region. It was almost like being in the Middle East with the flat-roofed mud-walled houses, and a wall all the way around the city. We visited the market which was a fascinating place – and contained everything you could think of from rubber tyres and Japanese cloth to sugar cane. I was most interested in the spices which were in heaps in front of the stalls. They had piles of stones which we were told they used in cooking – some might have been impurified rock salt and there was potash and alum. They also sold antimony – a shiny soft metal for decorating women's eyes. There were money changers who would take almost anything of silver or gold for money. A favourite form of currency was large silver coins made in Austria in 1780 from the Austro-Hungarian Empire, with the head of St Theresa on them. We passed men dying cloth a deep blue in vats in the ground, the smell of which was overpowering. I bargained for some leather goods in the market and bought a camel-skinned handbag for £2 to take back for my mother. We also visited the large mosque where we were allowed up a minaret and saw a terrific view of the town. We could see into the courtyards of the houses where the women spent most of their time. In those days, things were much more relaxed than now with regards to religious constraints.

On our various trips to Kano and to the East to Emugu the local people would wave to us, not uncommonly while they were relieving themselves on the side of the road laughing their heads off. Public toilets were in short supply as exemplified by a notice outside the post office from where you collected your post which said "please do not urinate here". Our VW Beetle did us proud when we had to

Kano Market

drive over lumps of rock that were not yet flattened into a road and we had to drive through the bush. It seemed more tolerant of the conditions than the British Land Rover and was only slightly inferior to a Peugeot 302*

One of the commonest sites on the alleyways of Kano were people with no fingers, hands or feet, or who were deformed in some other way, all due to leprosy. This disease is not highly infectious and only passed from person to person by intimate contact and can therefore be totally eliminated. The BCG vaccine against tuberculosis is thought to give some protection as the infection concerned is the same as the one that causes leprosy, that is, they are both mycobacteria. It seemed less common in the south although we knew of one settlement about 60 miles from Lagos in a town called Abeokuta. We paid several visits taking some of the sixth form boys with us who had never been before. The community was organised

---

* When I came back to England and we lived in Salisbury, I bought a small Peugeot and it was one of the worst cars I ever bought!

English engineer who after retirement had gone to his
d he wanted to do something useful and did he have any
somehow he ended up in Nigeria. When he first got
there the place was in disarray and no one was caring for the people.
He'd promised them that if they could make an effort he would help
them to get electricity laid on, clean running water and so forth, so
that at least their lives would be improved. Because of the prejudice
and fear engendered by this disease, the local people were very much
against it and would try to disrupt it by throwing bits of paper
over the wall on which were marked various 'juju' curses. Whereas
we would pick up and dispose of these messages, we noticed that
none of the boys would touch any of them, even though they came
from a Christian school situated in a modern major city. It was an
interesting example of the power of superstition.

The Hausas in Kano have a reputation for fighting and we
saw several men on horseback wearing brightly coloured robes and
swords. When we stopped in Zaria on the roadside for something to
eat, we were immediately surrounded by locals who seemed to arrive
from nowhere but just stood and watched us. This happened several
times later on in the tour and since we could not speak one another's
language, we just looked at each other. Sometimes we gave them
bread, which they took with great satisfaction. I can imagine they
thought we were as unusual as we did of them.

The other main tribe in the North are the Fulanis, who are
mainly cattle herders and the women wear large numbers of beads
round their necks. Some of the older ones wore only leaves. We
left Zaria for Jos which is on a plateau 4000 ft up. The Plateau was
very flat and surrounded by hills and the villages were surrounded
by fences of cacti which made them quite attractive. From Jos, we
went to Makurdi – 200 miles of laterite road which covered us with
dust. Sometimes we were driving round hairpin bends up hills, other

times we drove through inches of sand with the car sliding all over the place. It was great fun but very dusty. When we arrived at Makurdi we found there was no accommodation at the Rest House. The Arnolds* had a room in the Railway Rest House which was a bit bare but quite clean and we slept on camp beds they put up in the lounge for us. From Makurdi we crossed the Benue River and entered the Eastern region ending up staying at Enugu. The east is very clean and we were glad to see the deep green of the rain forest instead of the dry grasslands of the North. We visited Nsukka University which is an enormous campus but looked a bit like a factory site.

On another of our trips north we had to cross the river on a bridge that took trains and cars. While we were waiting for a train to pass one of the officials came and talked to us, finding that we were teachers said "oh you've come to help us" and he took us to his control room to show us around. The next trip we planned, two of us had hoped to visit Timbuktu but there was fighting on the border.

Dahomey

We did however get to Dahomey, a one-time French colony (now called Benin). They had built a new palace for the president in the capital of Benin and as he insisted that the marble for the floors should be air freighted from Italy, he broke the bank and ended up in jail. There were also hidden microphones all over the palace so that they could hear what people were saying. There was nothing happening in the palace when we were visiting, other than a few

---

* Mr Ajepway – the Nigerian art master visited the Arnolds when he came to the UK. They decided to pay a visit to the beach as they lived on the East Coast, and as they were sitting there on the beach in the cold wind with the sand blowing into their sandwiches Ajepway said "why do you come here?" It was a case of 'mad dogs and Englishman' but without the midday sun.

guards and ourselves so we were able to wander around at will. The old palace of Dahomey had walls made of mud and the blood of prisoners and there were eight thrones, each one mounted on four human skulls – not a happy place to be. One good thing about Dahomey was that the roads were beautifully tarmacked and kept in good condition, unlike those in Nigeria.

In her book, Lady Lugard, the wife of Lord Lugard Governor General of the West African Territories that covers most of the Sahara and surrounding territories, she outlines a detailed history of the various tribes.* There seems to have been a constant war between the Hausas and the Dahomey people. When the latter were in charge they were a particularly cruel and vengeful people whose activities are best left undescribed. Whereas the Hausas seemed to operate within a more civilised fashion. It seems to be forgotten in the discussions of slavery that although the colonial powers bought slaves, they were supplied by the African chiefs who were in charge. The slave traders were susceptible to yellow fever and malaria so couldn't go inland, which is one reason why the tribes were involved in bringing people to them. What is also forgotten is the appeal by David Livingston (the explorer), for commerce and business to be opened up in Africa in the hope that this would stop slavery.

In all our travels people were very grateful, and open to us. The only time there was tension was when the Principal of our school, arranged for us to go to a Rotary meeting in a hotel in Lagos. The English members of this Rotary group turned their backs on him and us. I felt very sorry for him, because he was extremely embarrassed and this seemed to me typical of the way some English people behaved abroad. I was therefore not surprised to observe over the time we were there, that German and French companies were

* 'A Tropical Dependency' by Flora L Shaw (Lady Lugard) 1905

displacing the sales of British goods and machinery. In addition, the English did not seem to work very hard and seemed to think they were superior to the locals and became snobbish and arrogant. This general attitude was not helped by the well-known British historian Arnold J Toynbee, who had been invited to give a lecture on the role of Africa in world history but really had nothing to say on the matter other than a few words about human evolution based on the finding of human bones in East Africa. He seemed unaware of the Nigerian bronzes of Eastern Nigeria. The Nigerian Attorney General who was chairing the meeting was clearly and understandably very cross and prevented the learned professor from answering any questions. This was the only occasion I can remember when there was a sense of interracial tension. We left the room in a hurry; it was very upsetting.

Eventually, the time came to return to England at the end of our contracts and we took one of the last sailings for the 11,000-ton vessel, the MV Apapa to Liverpool. When we left the dock at Lagos, they played all the 1960's music and at the end of the party on the ship, there was tear-jerking music by the New Seekers. In Bathurst the last African port, we left the radio officer behind after going on land, and he had to catch a lift on a small boat back to us. We had cabins, but the locals slept under a large tarpaulin with their chickens and goats, to get to the next port. We stopped at various other ports such as Takoradi (Ghana), Bathurst (now Banjul in The Gambia) and Las Palmas and a week or two later, came within sight of the cloudy grey, windswept Liver buildings in Liverpool.

The Return: Malaria and Marriage

On returning from Nigeria in 1965 I realised that the teaching profession was not for me. Having seen the burden of disease affecting children in Africa particularly those with malaria, I concluded that research into diseases of children in Africa was what I wanted to do. The World Health Organisation (WHO) states that: "there were an estimated 229 million cases of malaria worldwide. Children aged under 5 years are the most vulnerable group affected by malaria; in 2019, they accounted for 67% (274 000) of all malaria deaths worldwide."

Not long after my return there was an advert in *The Observer* newspaper for a research assistant to work on the development of a malaria vaccine, so I applied for the post and was delighted to be appointed. On reflection, it was surprising that I got the job as already indicated I did not get a first-class degree, coupled with the fact that I had spent 3 years out of academic work by doing my PGCE in Bristol and then teaching in Nigeria. My uncle Herbert once asked me what I was doing when I had returned, and I said I was at Guy's Hospital Medical School, to which he replied "Oh, you're still at school then?"

The girl from Johannesburg

It was not long after starting my PhD that I met my wife to be, Sue, in 1966. She had been in England for four years working as a primary school teacher and had planned to go back to her home in South Africa for good. When she had learnt that her eldest sister, Janet, was getting married she booked her return journey by boat – one of the last passenger boats from South Africa; the SS Orannje. We had only known each other a few months after meeting at St Mary's church in West Kensington. This time the Ford Anglia came in useful for transporting young ladies as well as monkeys.

Sue had a room on the first floor of one of the terraced houses in Gunterstone Road. One Sunday evening, after church, returning to her flat she realised she had forgotten her keys. But as this was not unusual, she had developed a knack of getting in through a window. However, on this occasion she misjudged her leap into the air and descended rapidly to the basement, which broke her fall and nearly her ankle, hit her jaw on a window sill and sustained various other minor cuts and bruises. This happened before I had met her so it

Miss Miller, the girl from Johannesburg

was several weeks later and she was still limping, I offered to take her home from church. So that was how it began.

Our experiences of Africa, although very different, meant that we had a common love for and interest in the continent and its people. The nearer it came to her return to South Africa, the less we liked the idea of being parted. But as everything was arranged, we eventually had to say goodbye at Southampton docks which was not romantic at all. I was so distressed I drove my Anglia at 90 miles an hour all the way home (or what seemed like it – I don't think it actually went that fast!). We kept in touch by airmail letters, thin sheets of light blue paper that didn't weigh much, as nobody had the internet or even a reliable land line (yes, such times existed). I suppose I should've said let's get married either in South Africa or England during the correspondence, but marriage is a big step and not something into which I had done any research. Eventually, Sue's father said to her "go back to England and see if you want to marry him or not", and "it's not necessarily if you can live with him, but whether you can live without him". So, one sunny autumnal evening I waited at Gatwick airport a couple of months later, for this Super Constellation, a four engine propeller passenger aircraft and saw this little lady in a red coat and a white hat descending the stairs from the aircraft and we fell into each other's arms – as you do. I was still unsure what to do next being a novice in these situations, but she said "if you don't marry me, I'm going back home". I said that "I had these monkeys to look after and was very busy, but shall we get married in April?" But Sue didn't want to wait that long, and persuaded me that we should get married before Christmas, so we had to get a special licence which gave us two weeks to organise it. When we told my mother we wanted to get married in two weeks' time she went into shock. When my father came home, she told him to "prepare himself for a shock". Sue had been staying in the front

Our 50th wedding anniversary in December 2016

room of a friend and I didn't have anywhere to live, having given up a church flat. Anyway, we had a small wedding, that someone remarked was the best one he'd ever been to because there were no speeches! We then spent a couple of days in a hotel in the Earl's Court area, while we looked for somewhere to live.

Affording a Ford

Eventually we found a ground floor flat in Fulham in a house owned by an old Baptist couple for three pounds a week. We were there for about 3 years while Sue had odd jobs, one working in the office at Lions, while I finished my PhD and we later had two children. I could hardly afford to run the Ford Anglia but discovered that the Salvation Army sold insurance policies and if you were teetotal, you got it cheaper, so sadly, no more gin and tonics. When my boss offered me some wine at the Christmas party, (incidentally in the absence of any wine glasses we drank out of beakers, acid cleansed of the radioactive monkey blood), I had to confess that I wasn't allowed any alcohol. He was horrified and said "we'll have to raise your salary!" Which is what happened, and we bought our first house in Blagdon Road, New Malden.

A very small car

When our son was a baby, they diagnosed a slight heart murmur which resulted in us going to an appointment with a leading paediatrician at Fulham hospital. When we turned up, there was a group of about 20-30 medical students being put through their paces by this illustrious gentleman. Michael was quite contented sitting on my knee, sucking his dummy which the doctor suggested we should quietly dispose of. Had I removed the dummy Michael would have

Ford Anglia: transport for ladies and monkeys. Drawing by Philip Castle, 2021

screamed his head off and then he would have understood why I hadn't 'disposed' of it. The medical students were then asked questions by the doctor, not really concerning the disease, but whether they could spell words like 'diarrhoea' which I felt rather unnecessary, but so it went on and I started to feel rather embarrassed for the medical students. He then asked me what I did for a living, so I said I was "working on the immunology of malaria" where upon Dr X said to the students "I expect this man knows more about immunology than you lot put together". At this point I decided I wanted to get away as quickly as possible – even more so when he suggested we should make another appointment to see him. I started to make our excuses as to why we couldn't go again and he wanted to know where we lived. When I said New Malden, he said "I live in New Malden, that's not very far", where upon my brain shut down and I said the daftest thing I have ever said which was: "I've only got a very small car". I don't know what happened after that, but we were determined never to see this pompous man again. I hope the medical students had a good laugh though! If ever I am tempted to rise above my station, I remind myself of this episode, which still amuses me 50 years later.

The Good Life

This was about the time of the television programme the "Good Life" and being a country lad at heart, I got an allotment plus chickens and a cockerel in the back garden. I used to take the children up to the allotment in the wheelbarrow and then when we got there Helen would need the toilet, but wouldn't do it behind the bushes, so had to take her all the way home again. (I'm told, she's the same now!). When we did manage to spend time there, we benefitted from blackberries, potatoes, leeks and endless runner beans.

This was also when Dr Denis Burkett was touring the country telling us all to eat bread made from stoneground flour with its high fibre content. I heard his lecture at Guy's hospital, and asked him if the large amount of salad the Americans ate was just as effective as the bran, but he said the Americans were the most constipated nation on earth. As you couldn't buy stone ground wholemeal flour in the shops, we had 70 pound bags delivered from a farm in Yorkshire, and we used to supply interested friends. The drivers who delivered these bags were always looking for a butcher's shop because they couldn't believe that anyone would want 70 pounds of flour unless they were a shop of some sort. I used to make two rather heavy, high fibre content loaves a week, and when I told my mother she said "I used to make 25" – so wasn't particularly impressed by my culinary achievements. In our efforts to remain healthy with our whole food diet, we also found a shop that sold nuts and seeds and fed the children peanuts as soon as they could chew anything which were referred to as "nuts a wuncy" (nuts and raisins). This possibly had the result of freedom from any peanut allergies, which meant we were well ahead of the research today that shows reduced risk of allergy problems later in life by early exposure to nuts and dirt (such as soil in the garden and the allotment). The old saying "eat a peck of dirt before you die" may have some truth in it. The adverts for detergents and cleaning agents that kill 99% of all known germs may be doing us more harm than good.

We fed our chickens wheat, as well as green scraps so we had eggs with nice yellow yolks. One of Helen's first "essays" was "I felt an egg and it was wom". We had a cockerel we called 'Early Bird' because he used to crow at 3 o'clock in the morning. This was rather early and we became concerned about waking the neighbours, so I took him to the animal house at Guy's – his fate remained unknown. However, far from complaining, the neighbours said they missed Early Bird as he made them feel as though they were in the countryside. Sadly, the chickens were killed by a fox when we let our house to tenants after we moved to Salisbury. It had been good experience for the children, learning where food came from and the organisation of the "class system" of chickens – with one poor soul called Silly Sally at the bottom of the scale.

Back to Business — Malaria

My limited experience of Africa plus a good deal of reading about tropical disease left me in no doubt of the importance of the project I was undertaking at the London School of Tropical Medicine. It was obvious that this was going to be a lifetime's work because at that time there were no vaccines for parasitic infections in humans and hardly any in animals, so this was attempting to break new scientific ground. All vaccines currently in use are for viruses and bacterial infections, all of which are much simpler and have fewer genes than *Plasmodium*, the parasite that causes malaria. The project was devised by Professor Sydney Cohen, Guy's Hospital Medical School and Professor Percy Garnham at the London School of Hygiene and Tropical Medicine and Dr Jim Fulton*. Professor Cohen's experience in immunology and Professor Garnham's vast experience of malaria and Dr Fulton's extensive experimental experience of working with malaria was a unique combination of talents. The research plan was based on the results of a small trial on children previously done by Cohen and McGregor in The Gambia. The trial involved treating children with high concentrations of antibodies to malaria isolated from serum from adults who had clearly become immune to the

---

* Dr Fulton (1899-1974) had worked with Sir Rikard Christopher (1873-1978), who was the oldest man in the Royal Society and died at 104. Cohen 1921-2017, Garnham 1901-1994 and McGregor 1922-2007.

disease. The trial was successful, though protection was temporary but this laid a basis for further work that could eventually lead to a vaccine. Obviously this could not be done in humans and therefore a suitable animal model as close to humans as possible was required. It was decided to use rhesus monkeys (*Macaca mulatta*) and a species of malaria called *Plasmodium knowlesi*. In the 1930's Coggeshall and Kum* obtained a similar result protecting the rhesus monkey, but used whole serum, as the method for isolating antibodies had not been developed.

The disease: background and history

The symptoms associated with the disease malaria are well-known: an especially high fever, followed by a cold phase with profuse sweating, rigours, headache, aching limbs, anaemia and a wide variety of acute conditions which sometimes lead to an incorrect diagnosis from typhoid to appendicitis.[†] Malaria also causes weight loss in a foetus and sometimes results in miscarriage. The main cause of death in children in Africa, usually aged between two and three, is cerebral malaria, traditionally thought to be the result of the parasitised red cells blocking the circulation of blood in the brain. While it has retreated from the outer regions of its maximum distribution (from Finland to Australia), it is still one of the most important of the many parasitic infections common to tropical and sub-tropical regions. Recently, it has been shown that *P. knowlesi*, our chosen parasite, infects people in forested areas of South East

---

* 'Demonstration of passive immunity in experimental monkey malaria' 1937, Coggeshall LT, Kumm HW. This was the first demonstration of antibody-mediated protection in malaria.
† See Peters and Gillies.

Asia. The species of *Plasmodium*, the parasite mainly responsible for mortality in humans is *Plasmodium falciparum,* although the other species can cause death (*see table*), generally, they have a much lower mortality. Nevertheless, they can make you very ill with repeated exposure, but patients who survive a number of attacks gradually become immune. Immunity in humans is species specific so that immunity to one species does not give immunity to another. Under natural circumstances, it takes several years for children to develop enough antibodies against different strains of *falciparum* malaria, such that they are eventually protected as adults. Malaria is thus a complex disease caused by a parasite with three different phases, the mosquito stage, the liver stage and the blood stage.

Table 1: characteristics of the five human malarias

Species of parasite	P. falciparum	P. vivax	P. ovale	P. malariae	P. knowlesi
Period of development in liver (days)	6	8	9	13	8
Length of a single blood cycle (hours)	48	48	48	72	27
Period between first infection and parasites detectable in blood (days)	9-10	11-13	10-14	15-16	9
Period between first infection and apperance of symptoms (days)	9-14	14 (or longer)	17 (or longer)	28 (or longer)	6-7
Severity of illness	Severe	Severe	Mild	Mild	Mild to severe
Mortality	Up to 20%	Occasional	None	Occasional*	Occasional
Geographic occurrence	Tropics, subtropics	Tropics, subtropics & temperate	Africa, Western Pacific	Patchy-in Africa, Asia	SE Asia
Drug resistance	Common	Occasional** to primaquine	None	Not significant	unknown
Persistence as "silent" forms in liver or blood	None	Up to 3 years in liver	Up to 3 years in liver	Up to 50 years (? In blood)	unknown
First discovered***	1880-1885	1880-1886	1900-1922	1880-1889	1932

*Some children die of kidney failure with persistent P. malariae.

**New evidence suggests occasional resistance to chloroquine.

***Period over which first seen and eventually described.

The Italian word for this condition, was thought to be due to 'bad air' from swampy ground – hence '*mal-aria*'. In many places these two features went together. In England, before the term malaria came into use it was called 'the ague'. In the account by Dr Thomas Sydenham who worked and published in the seventeenth century in London, all the symptoms of the agues are described and clearly relate to malaria.* It wasn't until the nineteenth century that *Plasmodium* was discovered when microscopes with sufficient power of magnification became available, along with the discovery of dyes that would stain cells for enhanced visibility.

The connection between the disease, and the microscopic organisms that we now know are one-celled parasites, was made by Alfonse Laveran, a French army doctor in Algeria.[†] The means by which malaria is transmitted was discovered by Ross and Manson.[‡] Manson had already demonstrated that mosquitoes could transmit a worm infection through previous work in China, although he was working in London at this time and is regarded as the founder of research of tropical medicine. When Ross, an army doctor, was on leave from India he met Manson who encouraged Ross to look for malaria in mosquitoes. Initially, the problem was that they didn't know what to look for. Ross observed the particles of brown pigment that malaria produces in the red cell of bird malaria and he followed this through by looking at the fate of this pigment in mosquitoes that had fed on a bird with malaria. Subsequently, Ross found the same result with mosquitoes fed on patients with malaria. This important discovery, for which Ross got the Nobel prize (but not Manson[§]), opened the

---

* Sydenham 1624-1689, was one of the founders of more scientific medicine including the use of Cinchona bark for treating malarial symptoms.
† For which he received the Nobel Prize. Lavern 1845-1922
‡ Ross 1857-1932, Mansen 1844-1922
§ It's unknown why the prize wasn't given to both parties.

possibility of preventing malaria through the control of mosquitoes. When Manson presented these results at meetings in London, some of the audiences were sceptical and said he was "a drunken Scotsman".* As with many new discoveries this kind of response was not surprising.

There are many host species infected with *plasmodia*. In addition to the five infecting humans, *Plasmodium* infects monkeys, birds, snakes, mice, rats and various other animals, though not most carnivores or ungulates (e.g. cows, goats, horses etc).† Prof. Garnham reported finding only one hippopotamus with malaria after looking through 137 slide specimens, which were all negative.

Mr Howard

The full completion of the life cycle was demonstrated through the courage of a volunteer, Mr Howard, a 39 year-old merchant seaman, who entered the portals of The London School of Hygiene in August 1949. In the paper 'The pre-erythrocytic stage of *Plasmodium falciparum*' it says:

> "Mr C.H. Howard earns both our gratitude and our admiration for the selfless part he played in offering himself for this experiment and for submitting cheerfully to all its requirements in order to further scientific knowledge in the hope that his action would eventually benefit others".

---

* Malaria seems to have attracted strong minded military types, namely Col. J A Sinton, an Irishman, the only fellow of the Royal Society with a Victoria Cross.

† One of my first papers was the discovery that the merozoites (see diagram) of *Plasmodium* were unable to attach to the red cells of resistant species. If we had thought about it more carefully we should have used the observations of red cells of different species and I think we might have made more progress towards a vaccine.

Volunteering to be a guinea pig for research on malaria a year before the experiment was performed, he put his arm into a cage with mosquitoes infected with human malaria (*Plasmodium falciparum*) over the course of three days and received 770 infected bites. The bites were treated with antihistamine and calamine lotion and 1% phenol solution. On the fourth day, they took 100ml of blood and injected it into another volunteer. After about one week a three quarter by one quarter inch of his liver was removed, fixed, sectioned and stained to reveal the presence of parasites. He began to show signs of malaria fevers and his red cells were parasitised so he was treated with chloroquine which cured the disease. This, demonstrated the complete lifecycle of a human malarial species. Other volunteers and monkeys were infected with different species of malaria to confirm these results of the lifecycle characteristic of *Plasmodium*.* The timing of these different phases, the blood phase, mosquito phase and liver phase (pre-erythrocytic stage) varies with each different species of host and parasite (*see table*). Most people have heard of someone getting malaria and having been treated and recovered may be free of the disease for months or even years until suddenly it returns.† In two human species this is due to the hypnozoite, which can remain dormant for long periods in the liver for reasons that we don't yet understand.

Malaria can also be passed from person to person simply by injecting a small amount of infected blood in the absence of a

---

* The discovery of the liver stage contradicted the work of Shaudin, and Austrian biologist, who claimed that the sporozoites went straight to the red cells.
† An apparently healthy lady who had had malaria in the past, was a blood doner. The recipient contracted malaria from her donation, even though it was 40 years since the doner had been infected. This was an unusually long time between the mosquito bite and becoming infectious. More commonly the time gap (pre-patent period) is months rather than years.

mosquito. In the past people got malaria from blood transfusions or even when a small amount of blood was injected by accident from a nurse or doctor in the course of diagnosis (e.g. if the patient was shivering a needle might slip and pierce their skin by accident).

Malaria as treatment

In 1917 the Austrian psychiatrist Wagner von Jauregg observed that people with syphilis, in which the brain has become infected, resulting in forms of 'madness', seemed to get some relief from this terrible condition if they developed a fever. This eventually led to patients being given malaria as this generates high fevers. Although there has been much discussion as to whether this really helped,

Temperature chart of neuro syphilis patient; drug treatment in red, black dots indicate temperature

it came to be generally accepted that this was a useful treatment and hospitals were established where malaria could be given to patients either by injections of blood or more commonly through mosquitoes. Hospital units were established in mental hospitals and one was The Mott Clinic in Horton hospital, Surrey.

Life-cycle of malaria*

The parasite

The life-cycle of the malaria parasite is complicated, consisting of three phases or cycles of development. A detailed description of the life history is given with figure 1, and interested readers may like to refer to this. However, to understand the nature of the problems associated with the disease, some knowledge of the parasite is necessary, and a brief outline of its life cycle is presented here.

It is convenient to begin the story with the parasites in the mosquito. Only female mosquitoes feed on blood and these have to be the right species to transmit malaria. When a mosquito bites its mammalian host, it first injects some saliva into the wound; this prevents the blood from clotting as it is sucked up through the multi-channelled proboscis into the mosquito's stomach. If malaria is present in this saliva, the parasites pass into the bloodstream. Those that reach the liver enter the cells of this organ and begin the "liver phase" of development. Each individual parasite multiplies within its host liver cell up to 40,000 times, over a period of one to two weeks, depending on the species (table 1).

---

* The life cycle taken from "Malaria; The intelligent traveller's guide, G A Butcher 1990". Immunology and malaria in general is a very complicated story. In addition to some very helpful general books, the publication "Essential Malariology" has up to date information with recent advances for those who want more detailed information.

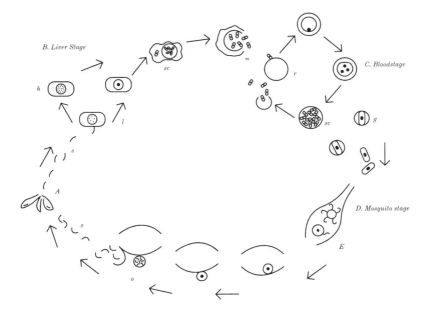

Figure 1 Life-cycle of malarial parasites in humans.

Each stage of the parasite is described by particular biological terms – but they are still Plasmodium. Parasites present as sporozoite(s) in the salivary glands of the mosquito (A) pass down the proboscis, which penetrates the skin. They are carried by the blood to the liver (B) and enter the liver cells (l) where they develop to become schizonts (sc). In P. vivax and P. ovale they may remain in arresting phase as hypnozoites (h) and commence development to schizonts later. The schizonts burst liberating merozoites (m) which begin the blood cycle (C) by penetrating the red cells (r). Multiplication of a single parasite within each red cell produces schizonts (sc) which burst liberating more merozoites to continue the blood cycle (each cycle takes 24, 48 or 72 hours). Some parasites develop to form gametocytes (g) beginning the phase of sexual reproduction (D). Fertilisation occurs within the mosquito (E), an oocyst (o) is produced, from which more sporozoites (s) are eventually generated.

The liver cell eventually bursts, liberating thousands of parasites into the blood. Each parasite is capable of invading the red cells present in the blood; these are the cells responsible for carrying oxygen around the body and contain the pink pigment haemoglobin. The invading parasites feed on the contents of the red cells and go through another phase of multiplication. This time, each parasite gives rise to 10 to 20 offspring within each red cell, and the period required for development is only 24, 48 or 72 hours (see table 1). The red cells burst and the young parasites are again liberated into the bloodstream. They invade more red cells and the process is repeated. Thus, every two to three days a new brood of parasites is produced in the blood and more red cells become infected. The bursting of many red cells to liberate their contents initiates the fevers that appear every two to three days in malaria patients.

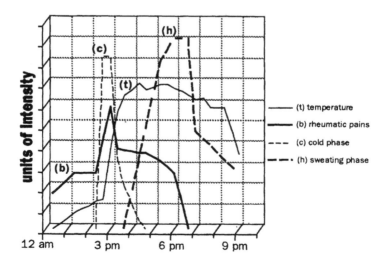

Graph showing symptoms of mild attack of P. vivax

Some parasites do not multiply within the red cell but become sexual stages. The so-called "male" parasite (*microgametocyte*) produces the sperm-like forms which fertilise the "female" gamete (*macrogametocyte*). Thus, fertilisation occurs in the insect's stomach. The parasites pass through the stomach wall and form a cyst, within which more cell division takes place. Eventually, the parasites within the cyst pass to the mosquito's salivary glands and are ready to infect a new mammalian host. The life-cycle is thus completed.

The liver stages of malaria parasites are relatively few in number, as many of the invading forms from the mosquito are destroyed by the body's defences, particularly the "white cells".

The liver stages cause no symptoms and an infected person is unaware of the presence of malaria parasites. Only when the blood is infected do symptoms become noticeable.

One Project, Two Bosses

Work at the London School of Hygiene and Tropical Medicine

The purpose of our experiments was to use the model by Cohen and McGregor to eventually discover the proteins of the malarial parasite that stimulated the production of protective antibodies. Protection was demonstrated in children as they were cured of the infection although the effect was temporary. We aimed to replicate this approach using monkeys in the hope that this would lead to the development of a vaccine. As per Cohen and McGregor, we collected serum from monkeys immune to malaria; in our experiments monkeys were infected but drug treated so that they became immune. This type of experiment is called passive immunity as the antibody fraction of the serum, isolated by a simple chemical procedure, was not produced in the children themselves and disappeared after a week or two.

On my first day at the London School, I was greeted by the chief technician who said he was not interested in this project. To be fair, I think he had enough to do as it was, since Professor Garnham was not terribly interested in the practical day to day running of his department and as I got to know the situation better it was clear that he was very demanding but perhaps had little idea of the work load on the staff. He was even unaware of how many monkeys he was using. On one occasion, he wanted three more monkeys to infect with another species of *Plasmodium*. However, the chief animal technician, Jim, told him there was no space for more monkeys in the animal house. Garnham was a bit irritated and asked whose monkeys were taking up the space. Jim then went through the list and in most cases staff had two or three each. When it came to Garnham's name, he had considerably more monkeys than the rest (from memory, 47) which he had probably used at one stage, but had forgotten about and were now growing old and fat!

Garnham: Boss 1: malaria and monkeys

Because Garnham was often abroad (probably chasing parasites in some far off jungle), and was internationally recognised, he had many visitors, some of whom were also very distinguished but unknown to us newcomers.* He was not concerned, as some heads of research groups were, about people stealing his ideas and passed the frequent visitors on to us PhD students with the instructions to tell them what we were doing. An American visitor sat politely listening to me, a novice, explaining the life cycle of malaria; I looked blankly at the visitor as Garnham introduced him, but he held out his hand and said "you don't have to know me". He was an eminent professor, who later became a friend for life.

Garnham may have appeared to be an 'absent minded professor',† but apparently he could have been a concert pianist had he not chosen a scientific career and I suspect, had a subtle sense of humour. When he was in colonial service in East Africa his job was officially

---

* Apart from myself, the other PhD students were from Malaysia, Sudan and Kenya.

† If you met Garnham in the corridor he would stop and ask you about your results, whereby he would stare into space and then suddenly wander off leaving you standing, without commenting.

Professor PCC Garnham FRS, photo: courtesy of the RSTMH

checking customs forms and other documents. If they arrived when he was playing tennis he would send his wife to sign the forms. Unsurprisingly, the authorities were not impressed. Garnham's lack of awareness of the cost of running a department was exemplified by his habit of crossing diamond pencils off the equipment list because he thought they would be expensive.* But his book on malaria was so detailed and comprehensive and beautifully produced that to my mind it almost compares to a work of art as well as science. The pictures of malarial parasites were intricately painted by two ladies sitting at a microscope producing watercolour paintings, using brushes with no more than a few hairs. It is unlikely that anyone will ever produce a new edition. It covers everything from the common human malarias to *plasmodia* only observed once in a hippopotamus. It is the complexity of the life-cycle, the variation in the breeding habits of mosquitoes, environmental temperatures, differences in susceptibility of the different parasite stages to antimalarial drugs and so forth that makes the control and epidemiology of malaria so difficult.

Weighing fruit

My first attempt to infect monkeys in order to give them the appropriate dose of parasites required the monkeys to be weighed, but having started the procedure I could find no proper scales on which to weigh them. I hunted around for some weights, the minimum of which was 20 grams; using some grocer's scales and weighing whatever was available: a bag of sugar, apples and bananas to the nearest 20g. It says in the published paper that monkeys weighed 3.1

---

* At that time many of the staff had been doctors in the colonial service; in fact, one of the reasons for the School of Hygiene was to train doctors to go to the tropics.

to 3.2kg, but obviously this is not exactly what they weighed; on my count it was 2 bags of sugar, a bag of apples and a banana.

Exsanguination

Having dissected many animals in my zoology degree, bleeding live animals to get as much blood as possible was obviously a technique that needed to be mastered. I was shown by Dr Fulton how to do this on a monkey by opening the chest cavity, severing the aorta and sucking up the blood with a large syringe. This was a very messy process and as I was demonstrating it to another student, I pierced my finger with a scalpel blade. Had I been Colonel Knowles, I would have left it to see if I came down with malaria, but being of a nervous disposition and worried about viruses I had to report it to the Health and Safety department – which at that stage was the doorman – who simply plunged my hand into a bowl of detergent. When I told him I'd squeezed my finger to get the blood out, he said: "I'm glad you did that Sir". I'd phoned my wife Sue to say what I'd done and I was worried, but then went back to work. When I got home, I'd forgotten all about it but Sue was still worried stiff. As a result of this experience, I abandoned Dr Fulton's messy method and later got as much blood by cardiac puncture (and made a mental note not to tell my wife about mishaps unless it really was a problem …)

A royal visit

One morning when we arrived for work, we found that we had been moved to a new lab for a day before a visit from a member of the Royal Family. Pieces of new equipment suddenly appeared from nowhere, and subsequently disappeared again after the visit. We weren't introduced to HRH because as she stepped into the lab our

Malaysian student had a half-dissected rat in his hand, so she made a rapid retreat. That was the nearest I got to royalty.

The friendly cockroach

The School of Hygiene was founded in 1902 and had an international reputation for research on tropical disease, but not enough decent equipment. When I first started at LSH there was no protective clothing provided – no boots, gloves, or masks – and we were therefore exposed to a great deal of dust, not to mention that the floor of the animal house appeared to move as it was covered in cockroaches. These were a particular problem for me as they would suck the blood off the microscope slides before I had a chance to stain them. Also they would sit on the bridge of the microscope and tickle my forehead with their antennae (I think they were just being friendly). Insecticides were not allowed in the building as far as I can remember, because they might also kill the mosquitoes that were bred for research. They were grown in big bowls of water containing a lump of turf, in small rooms underneath Mallet Street.

Who's for DDT?

One of the last meetings of the Royal Society for Tropical Medicine near Portland Place that I can recall was a black and white film from the colonial era in which three medical officers were trying to persuade an African Chief that he should allow them to spray DDT (Dichlorodiphenyltrichloroethane), on the walls of the huts. DDT was still fairly new, but had been shown to protect people from malaria. The chief was not impressed so one of the English officers sprayed some mealy porridge with the sprayer and then ate the porridge. We think one of the doctors may have been Professor Garnham.

Coping with conferences

One aspect of research that I found difficult, for reasons already stated from my childhood, was attending scientific conferences. The first one that the boss had arranged for me and another PhD student to attend was a conference organised by the Spastics Society, at the Royal Spa Hotel Tonbridge Wells. The conference was entirely on immunology, a subject of which I still knew very little, as at that time it was taught in medicine but not in biology courses and I was also still trying to learn about malaria. As we approached a group of eminent medical scientists, suddenly a hand appeared from amongst the expensive suits and Harris Tweed jackets who arrived before us and a deep Italian voice said, "I am Ruggiero Ceppallini, I have just flown in from New York." Not to be outdone, I nearly replied; "I am Geoff, I have just come from Fulham, in my Ford Anglia". I managed to stop myself in time.

I came away from the conference perplexed and unenlightened and it took a long time before I felt comfortable in such erudite company, although people were generally pleasant. Compared to other aspects of malaria, there was very little research on immunology. In fact, I was told it was difficult enough to understand immune responses to a simple thing like a red cell, let alone a complex organism like a parasite. However, I received some encouragement at another meeting when I found myself trying to explain about our project to make a malaria vaccine to a Professor White, one of the founders of the British Society for Immunology. I suddenly realised that I was going to quote from the standard text at that time on immunology by Humphrey and White* when I realised I was sitting

---

* Dr Bob White was involved in the early trials of penicillin which had the unfortunate side effect of making him partially deaf. He mentioned also that he was watching the Battle of Britain while sitting in his garden reading the papers. He was the deputy Head of the Medical Research Council Laboratories at Mill Hill.

opposite Prof. White. His comment on our vaccine project was: "It should not be beyond the wit of man to make a vaccine against malaria" which provided a much-needed boost to my sagging morale. As he was giving his lecture, leaning on the long wooden pointer, on the edge of the stage, I remember thinking he was going to fall off. I'm glad he didn't – he seemed the typical absent-minded professor. During the main lecture he pointed out, "We don't really know what lymphocytes do." The subject has made rapid progress since those far-off days* and here we are fifty years later, "knowing what lymphocytes do" and with more than one type of vaccine on the cards.

How not to handle monkeys

When it came to working with monkeys the difficulties in getting the work done was not made any easier by the absence of regular technical assistance. Because the parasites multiplied every 24 hours I needed to take smears twice a day to know how much antimalarial drug (mepacrine), to keep the monkeys from getting sick, but also to allow the parasite to persist so they could become immune. In order to take a small blood sample from the ear of a monkey, it had to be held between the front of the cage and a false back so that it could not move. When it came to injecting some infected blood into the animal, we had to take the monkey out of the cage by pinning its arms and preventing its head from turning so it could bite you. This was a fairly scary experience for the person holding the monkey and positively terrifying to the monkey. I eventually discovered

---

* Lymphocytes are the most common white cells in the blood, constantly circulating throughout the body. If you have no lymphocytes, you have no immune response. The other group of white cells are the phagocytes which are larger. There are a number of different types and they are involved in 'gobbling up' bugs.

that this very harrowing method of getting monkeys infected was completely unnecessary as they could be sedated with a small dose of anaesthetic that would put them to sleep for 20 minutes. Officially I was not allowed any of the anaesthetic as it was said to be too expensive. My answer to this problem was to follow the example of my Leicestershire uncle, who was a poacher, to go in early and take whatever anaesthetic was needed. Obviously, this situation required a better solution.

Moving to Guy's

As this was a joint project between the London School of Hygiene and Guy's Hospital Medical School, the boss suggested I take whatever I needed from the stores in the department at Guy's so I filled my Ford Anglia with the anaesthetic, microscope slides, beakers and other glassware and whatever else I needed. Eventually, the bulk of the work shifted to Guy's; which also required moving the monkeys. So I anaesthetised them, put them in two plastic dustbins with holes in the lid, into the boot of my Ford Anglia. The biggest problem on arrival at Guy's was parking and the car park attendant. I didn't have a parking permit and neither did the monkeys. Happily, all arrived safely while they were still napping and were transferred to the appropriate part of the animal facility, temporarily in the same room as the baboons. This may sound very bizarre, but at the time the work needed to get done as quickly and efficiently as possible. Needless to say, it would not be done this way today.

Intelligent baboons

The baboons (*Papio papio*), were housed in cages on top of a trolley. By leaning with their back on one side and their feet on the other, they learnt to rock the cage so sometimes it would fall off the trolley and they could get out. They seemed to want to watch what we were doing, so this rocking would enable them to position their cages to look over our shoulders. One morning I went in and one baboon had a black eye. The technician had opened the gate then turned his back to pick up a cabbage to give him. The baboon started to get out so he socked him in the eye to get him back in the cage. As they had very long teeth, it would have been quite difficult and dangerous if they had got out. When I went in at weekends, I was warned to check the room was clear before I went in. Thankfully, this is not the way they are treated now – if in fact they are used at all.

Cohen: Boss 2

It became obvious when I started at the LSHTM, that I would have to get on with the job as best I could. I was given a rather inferior portable Russian microscope and as anyone will tell you, finding malaria parasites on a stained microscope slide can be quite difficult for the uninitiated if they are few in number.*

When we eventually moved to Guy's, we bought a new 'research' microscope. In contrast to Garnham, Sydney Cohen was more hands on, which I appreciated, although, sometimes it would have been better if he was more hands off! Sydney didn't know much about microscopes so he brought one of his colleagues from the medical school to check it over. When Sydney looked down it, he said he could see 'long black things', to which I replied "those are your eyelashes". On another occasion, when he came into the lab, he

---

* There are two sorts of blood film, thick and thin. We only checked the thick films when parasite numbers were extremely low and a drop of blood was not smeared on the slide, but left to dry as a droplet.

was showing a visitor how to label proteins with radioactive iodine, a technique he had used often. When he checked the bench at the end of the procedure with a Geiger counter to make sure he had not spilt anything, he found that the proteins were unlabelled, but one of his thumbs was radioactive which caused some merriment – not many people have a radioactive boss!*

Not being in *The Times*

Whether or not it was the same thumb that Sydney made radioactive, I don't remember, but whichever one it was, he somehow cut it with his lawnmower and it became infected. Far from being cleared up with antibiotics, he started getting rigors quite suddenly without warning and everybody kept asking him if he had malaria. He was due to give a talk at the British Association for the Advancement of Science in Lancaster, but he got half-way there and started to get sick again. So I was phoned up one weekend and asked "could I go to Lancaster straight away to get there in time to give the lecture?" and I managed to get a train that got me there with minutes to spare. I duly gave my lecture, and came home that evening but there was a problem on the trains so it took about eight hours to get home. I ended up with a bad headache which lasted for some time, and the lecture was reported in *The Times* although unfortunately, stating it was given by Prof. Sydney Cohen – not Dr. Geoff Butcher! Sydney eventually spent some time in hospital at Guy's and it seemed as though the surgeons wanted to chop his thumb off and the physicians wanted to find out what it was. Eventually, they removed a small splinter of bone in the wound and he was cured. His experience in hospital

---

* It didn't seem to worry him; he took iodine to counteract the radioactivity.

did not impress his notion of how the health service was run at that time having learnt his training in South Africa where they still had matrons who kept everybody in order.

Solvents and solutions

When we needed to sample from our cultures over a 24-hour period, Sydney volunteered to help with taking samples from the cultures through the night. When I tried to explain to him our techniques for avoiding contamination of the cultures, such as wearing masks and gloves etc, he was somewhat dismissive and said he knew all about that. It was no surprise to me to come in the following morning to see our cultures completely destroyed by bacteria. He wasn't the kind of chap to avoid admitting a mistake, so at least he was 'amenable to correction' and my respect and liking for him grew.

One afternoon, when I was quite glad Sydney was in the lab, his technician dropped a two and a half litre bottle of sulphuric acid which broke open. There were pools of acid attacking the floorboards and going black and her skirt was dissolving in no time at all. Fortunately, we had a lot of bicarbonate solution handy and poured it on the technician and the floor which bubbled and frothed like a witch's brew. At just that moment our cleaner – a ferocious lady known as Mrs 'Un – appeared at the door to the lab and said "oo's been making a mess of my floor?!" apparently not at all worried by the possibility of the technician being dissolved. Sydney was not impressed and said "Mrs 'Un, we've had a serious accident!". A few days later, he managed to find some dust in some obscure corner, about which he complained and she resigned, much to everyone's relief.

To measure parasite growth in cultures, we added a radioactive amino acid. Dick Crandle (a charming, good humoured, visiting

American) and I, attempted several different methods of processing the samples to count the radioactivity. One of which was putting malarial samples on filters and then into a solution based on toluene. The other method was to precipitate the proteins in the samples with acid and then dissolve the precipitate in an alkaline solution.*

On one occasion, when we had finished with the experiment and poured it down the sink, the toluene evaporated. When it went down the sink, it somehow gassed people in the floor below and they complained. So we had to find somewhere else to dispose of it and the most convenient receptacle was the nearby ladies toilet. Unfortunately, the Professor of Forensic Medicine employed his wife as his secretary (another ferocious lady). When she heard where the waste radioactive material was being disposed of, she was understandably less than happy and conveyed her righteous indignation to the Prof, who conveyed it to me. Eventually, the authorities provided the proper waste containers, as usual in my experience, behind the times. This is one occasion where I would say three cheers for Health and Safety. In another procedure I used ether as a solvent for a particular preparation without protection, when my wife said to me one day after I arrived home "you're breathing out ether". Apparently, ether tends to concentrate in the red cell membrane, and solvents unfortunately are one of the possible causes for Parkinson's disease.

---

* Unknown to me at the time, several years later, I discovered Sydney had taken the wrong column of data that was published in a Nature paper. As it happened, this didn't change the result, but they would have been more impressive had he taken the right figures. The reason I didn't spot it was because due to the pressure of time, I had already started another experiment. Other groups latterly carried out the same procedures to confirm our results, so the mistake wasn't significant.

Feeding monkeys fruit and some detective work

In order to study the possible interaction of antibodies and the parasite, we needed to get constant growth of the parasite in our cultures over one life cycle i.e. 24 hours. Although we used a standard culture media supplemented with rhesus serum, our initial attempts at culturing *Plasmodium knowlesi* failed – they simply died before completing a cycle of growth. Obviously, this was very frustrating as we couldn't study any effect of immune sera and antibodies unless the parasites grew normally. I took samples from the cultures and looked at the red cells under the microscope and found that instead of being a normal discoid shape the red cells were spherical with minor projections on the surface. In the medical literature, red cells of this shape were 'acanthocytic'. I read that red cells in patients with a disease called abetalipoproteinemia lacked the protein required to transport vitamin E round the body, although we had incorporated vitamin E to the culture medium without success. At this point I contacted Mill Hill MRC laboratories, the only place in the UK where they were working on this malaria. I discovered that their monkeys were given a pellet diet plus fruit, whereas our monkeys were only given a pellet diet. We then insisted that they were also given fruit, and as a result, we found our red cells from then on were the normal discoid shape. The parasites multiplied normally and we were able to do the work on immunology that we hoped would lead to a vaccine (and had happier monkeys). The vitamin E maintained the vitamin C in the red cell membranes which were then able to retain their normal shape and the parasite could enter and sustain normal growth. Once we managed to get the monkeys on the correct diet, with their coats looking shinier as well as their red cells in the right discoid shape, parasites developed and multiplied successfully. By 1970 we were able to show a good correlation between immunity

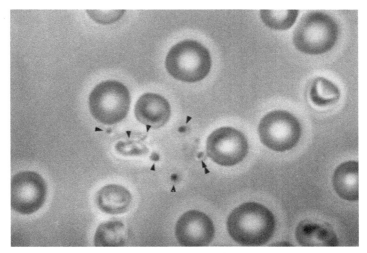

Still frame of merozoites just freed from schiozont (normal serum).
Photographs from G Butcher PhD thesis

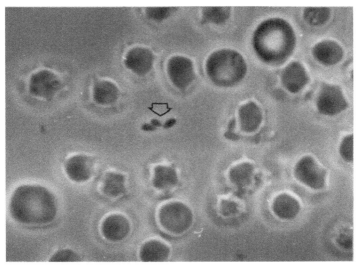

Still of schizoogny of P. knowlesi in immune serum
showing aggutinated merozoites

in our monkeys and inhibition of parasite growth in our cultures as measured by the uptake of the radioactive amino acid. We could observe these events under the microscope so with the help of Eric Tachell in the biology department, we made an 8mm black and white film of schizonts liberating merozoites. In the presence of normal monkey serum the merozoites attached to red cells and invaded them but in immune serum they agglutinated (stuck together) and failed to enter red cells.

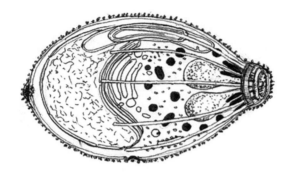

Diagram of a merozoite to show it's structure uniquely designed to enter a red cell. This picture was constructed from electron-micrograph photos of sections of the parasite. Picture courtesy: Prof. Lawrie Bannister

In the news – searching for a vaccine

By this time, around 1976, we had discovered that we could immunise monkeys with merozoites such that they would resist a high dose of *P. knowlesi* and show no signs of sickness. When these results were published, they were taken up by the media who interpreted the data as the possibility of a human malaria vaccine just around the corner. What they didn't report in most cases was the fact that these were whole parasites and they were mixed in a suspension of paraffin oil and dead mycobacteria called Freund's Complete Adjuvant (FCA).* We had people phoning up saying they were going to the tropics and wanted to be immunised with our vaccine. Unfortunately, this adjuvant tended to produce quite nasty ulcers at the point of injection, but if we had injected the merozoites alone, we would get no response. I had to explain all this in a broadcast at Bush House on the BBC World Service to a background of beating drums for "atmosphere". The interviewer wanted to know how long it would be before there was a malaria vaccine for Africa – I picked a figure out of my head and said "15 years" (not a very good guess!).

Bursting the red cell

A major contribution to this work was a cell-sieve that separated schizonts from merozoites in a culture vessel invented by our chief technician Dave Dennis. Although we only took out a preliminary patent, it was used by other malaria groups. Dr Lou Miller, the head of one of these groups said they could collect merozoites by the teaspoon full. The next phase of the operation was to try and identify those proteins in the merozoites that stimulated protective antibodies. Without going into a lot of details, we had two ways of breaking up cells of which one was called the 'French Press' and the other used a detergent called Lysolecithin.

Although the results of immunisations with the merozoites and FCA were encouraging in that the monkeys showed good immunity, this time the level of immunity did not corelate with the level of antibody

_____

* Originally developed by Dr Freund in the 1940's. An adjuvant is a substance used to enhance the body's immune response to improve the effectiveness of a vaccine. FCA is no longer used and better things have been produced, but at the time it was the only available adjuvant to us.

to parasites in their blood. Clearly the immune response that protected the monkeys was not due solely to antibodies. When we injected a very large number of *P. knowlesi* infected red cells (10^{10}) the monkeys not only resisted this massive challenge but we could see that the parasites inside the red cells were damaged (crisis forms), by some unknown mechanism. Further, when we injected parasites of a different species; *P. cynomolgi bastianellii*, they were also damaged; thus demonstrating that this immunity under these circumstances was non-specific.

Professor McGregor visited us at Guy's and asked me what crisis forms were (I was tempted to say "dear Professor McGregor, that is something you should have learnt at your mother's knee"); after spending thirty years of researching malaria in the Gambia he had never seen a crisis form as they are not seen in human malaria. This was the type of immune response that you can see in rodent species of malaria. By coincidence, this was when Ian Clark contacted us as they wanted some electron microscopy done on the rodent species by Lawrie Bannister at Guy's. We had also asked Lawrie to look at our parasites. This was the time when Ian and I had come to the same conclusions. I had been fascinated by crisis forms when I was starting to read about malaria in 1965 having read the first description of them by the Taliaferro's in 1937. This aspect of malaria on non-specific immunity is explained later in the work I did when I joined Ian in Canberra years later. Coincidentally, this was the first time we also gave Lawrie Bannister samples of merozoites combined with red cells for electron microscopy. This was the beginning of a long association that resulted in many studies on the biology of malaria.

Different strains

There was another problem in terms of developing a vaccine and this is a little bit complicated. Most people by now would have heard about

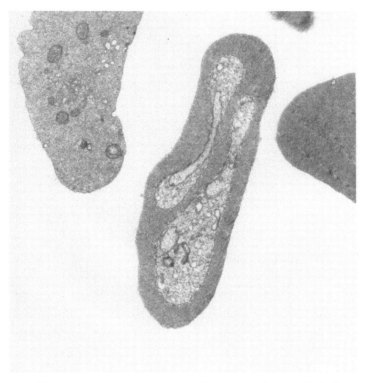

Electron-micrograph photo of a crisis form parasite showing a lack of structure (top left) compared to a normal parasite (centre of photo) within the red cell. Photo courtesy of Prof. Ian Clark

the Corona virus and the fact that it may produce different strains, the anxiety being that the vaccine might work against a normal strain, but not against a mutant strain. With the Corona virus this could take months or weeks. With malaria it happens within a week to get a new variant. It is the surface of the infected *schizont* where this occurs. Sydney didn't believe the parasite could change its antigens in this way, although he should have accepted it because it had already been demonstrated in sleeping sickness (*Trypanosomiasis*). His argument was that if you think that antigens can change, though they are no longer specific to a particular organism, you undermine the whole of immunology. He eventually came round to accepting antigenic variation and we set about the process of looking for antigens – beginning with breaking open the red cells to release the parasite. Our first effort was using the French Press.*

French Press

We had demonstrated that the antibodies to human and monkey malaria would attack the phase of the cycle called *merozoites* and stop them entering new red cells. Therefore, it was *merozoites* that contained the antigen and if you could identify and isolate the antigen you had a potential vaccine. Dave Dennis (the chief technician) and I, set about this with the intention of releasing the *merozoites* by breaking open the red cell membrane. Because these things are very tiny we tried using a high-pressure cylinder of air that forced the malaria parasites through a very small hole in a metal

---

* Some people did get very upset if their grant application was turned down if Sydney was chairing the committee but instead of taking it up with him, they'd phone me up, even though I was still quite a junior member of the establishment, and give me an earful of how wicked Sydney was. A more mature colleague told me to take it all with a pinch of salt, which I did.

tube. As it came out of the tube it expands automatically and the cells would burst open; this apparatus was called the 'French press' (like the coffee pot). When Dave switched the gas on to release the pressure I found I was looking at him through a pink cloud of haemoglobin, which happily disappeared rather rapidly. Dave said something about possible adjustments being needed.

Chemistry is cooking: a pinch of venom

Our next attempt, at the suggestion of Professor Geoffrey Webster,* at releasing the parasite from the red cells involved a chemical procedure starting with twelve eggs. We separated the yolks from the whites; which we put in the chromatography oven to make meringues. The yolks were homogenised (whisked) and treated with a range of solvents: methanol, ether, chloroform etc. Finally, we had a clear solution in a round bottom flask. We then added a pinch of snake venom and within a few seconds, a white precipitate appeared. This was a detergent, lysolecithin. When mixed with the infected red cells the detergent ruptured the red cell membrane, so releasing the *schizonts*. These were processed further to release a mixture of proteins, most of which would have been antigens. A few weeks later, I was looking in a chemical catalogue and realised I could have bought lysolecithin. But then we wouldn't have had meringues …

---

* A biochemist expert on lipids

WHO Goes Where?

From immunology to culture work

At a meeting of an expert committee on malaria at the World Health Organisation in 1974, one of the recommendations resulting from the discussions on what the next priorities should be in malaria research, was the emphasis on the need to maintain *P. falciparum* (human malaria) in continuous culture. Until this time, almost all the work on immunity to malaria focused on experimenting on rodents, birds and monkeys. Apart from obtaining small amounts of blood from patients, the only other source was to infect a species of South American monkey, but these were restricted to American researchers.

WHO expert committee, Geneva, 1974: from right: Sydney Cohen; Geoff Butcher; Geoff Target; Walter Wernscharfer. Photo G Vuarchex

After this meeting, Sydney, Graham and I decided we had to try and grow *P. falciparum* in culture as well as continuing the work on merozoites and vaccine development. As I had the most experience in culturing, it was decided that I would concentrate on that aspect. The Microbiological Research Establishment (MRE), at Porton Down, was constructed to deal with dangerous microorganisms that could have been used as biological weapons in warfare.* The MRE's purpose was gradually coming to an end and the unit was being converted to civilian use, which is why I was allowed to work there.† At Porton, they had a reputation for growing larger quantities of biological material than was possible in an ordinary lab and under secure conditions. Initially I would go down to Salisbury once a week, but this became impractical, so we decided to move the family to Salisbury.

Shaken not stirred

One of the most important breakthroughs in the story of malaria as such, was the development of a method for keeping human malaria going in perpetuity by Professor Bill Trager and Dr Jensen in New York in 1976.

---

* Often this site is confused with the Chemical Defence Establishment (CDE) by the media, which still operates under the MOD. Although they were no longer involved in defence against biological warfare, the MRE became a centre for dealing with new human infections. Teams of people were sent off to tropical areas to find the source of new diseases, 60% of which come from animals. In some cases, such as Lassa fever, they identified the multimammate rat as a source of infection. This type of work was obviously hazardous and some people received bravery awards. The work was not made easier by the need for staff to be wearing protective clothing which so frightened the villagers who ran away.

† It was interesting to see research being done in an establishment where everyone had secure jobs – they seemed to lack the excitement of discovery. One felt in labs where staff on short term contracts, they were more open to looking for new ideas within their limited timeframe.

I was probably the first person in this country to use this method to grow falciparum *in vitro*, using Trager's method as Sydney had just returned from New York with Trager's paper publishing the basic conditions for keeping these parasites multiplying and growing in 1978. I learnt later that I was somewhat unpopular with Professor Trager, because in his method petri dishes containing malaria were kept at 37°C in a candle jar. This was an old-fashioned method of growing bacteria in which you lit a candle in a sealed container such as a desiccator which contained less oxygen and more carbon dioxide. He was also insistent that the cultures should not be shaken or stirred. In my hands, the malaria grew much better in normal flasks in a shaking incubator and this was subsequently adopted by most research groups who wanted to obtain *P. falciparum* in quantity. The same method also worked with *P. knowlesi* in my hands.

Porton didn't allow a class II Laminar flow cabinet which is what other labs used, so I resorted to working on an open bench wearing a face mask, gloves and using a Bunsen burner and glass pipettes.* The only regular blood supply for the serum needed for culture that was available, was the outdated bags of blood donated from the local hospital. Red cells came from blood taken from staff volunteers. The initial malaria sample came from West Africa in liquid nitrogen, brought by my colleague Graham Mitchell. With my method I could obtain about a third of the red cells with parasites in reasonable shape. Surprisingly, different strains of falciparum cultured at the same time in the same medium, grew at different rates, but were consistent in their rate of growth and multiplication. The same culture method also worked with *P. knowlesi*. The method the Porton people used wasn't successful, so effectively I ended up working on my own, following my own method. The only advantage of working at the MRE was the

_____

* They insisted I use a class III cabinet for my work which was too inconvenient and not necessary.

ease of getting there. This was important as in the early days I needed to change culture media every eight hours. My children remember my absences as I was always "going to change the medium". As we wanted to obtain as much falciparum parasites as possible, various methods were tried to increase the volumes of material. To save doing it manually every few hours, I devised a simple, shaking flask, on a timer which became stationary to allow the red cells to settle over two hours before the old medium which by then was depleted of nutrients, was pumped off automatically and new medium pumped in.

I was the only person in the country culturing falciparum and had quite a few people who came to see how this was done, although I was still using traditional techniques with cultures on an open bench. I managed to establish the basic conditions for *P. falciparum* for asexual (blood) stages. Growing parasites for infecting mosquitoes required different conditions which I didn't become involved with until I worked at Imperial College years later.

By the time I came to the end of my period at Porton, I had published methods for continuous culture of *P. falciparum* and *P. knowlesi*.

Somewhere to live

*"Down in the jungle living in a tent: better than a pre-fab. No rent."**

We had to find somewhere to live in or near Salisbury that had a good train service to London and would also be convenient to Porton. We looked around the area and couldn't find anything, until someone suggested the Common Cold Research Unit called

---

* Charlie Chester

Michael, Sue and Helen outside our flat in Harvard Hospital

Harvard Hospital. As I was funded by the Medical Research Council (MRC) and so was the Research Unit, we got permission to move there at the beginning of 1977.

History of Harvard Hospital

This site was interesting accommodation as it was composed of about 40 asbestos huts that were sent to this country by Harvard University Medical School for wounded American and Canadian soldiers during the second world war. It was actually sent out twice as the first batch of nurses and huts was torpedoed. It was an institution quite unlike anywhere else in the UK. The huts were larger than the prefabricated huts we had in this country consisting of a long corridor of about 60 feet with rooms off this corridor on one side. Having been quickly built during the war, the walls of our 'hut' were fairly thin* which benefitted the children as they could look through holes (no doubt suitably enlarged by them), in the wall of their bedroom to watch our television next door. We would find notes slipped under the sitting room door to say we were lucky as "we could watch tv when we wanted".

After the war, the MRC decided to work on the common cold at the hospital as it was conveniently situated not far from Salisbury. Volunteers given the common cold virus, could be isolated and experiments involving transmission of the virus were done through a variety of approaches. They advertised for volunteers and at first they had problems getting enough people but employees from nearby factories came along and after that they had no difficulties recruiting people to help with the project. I should emphasise I was not involved with the common cold research; I continued my work on malaria at Porton Down.

The common cold: sneezing for science

Harvard Hospital became popular with students on vacation wanting to study without distractions and with board and lodging thrown in. After the war, honeymoon couples with little money were happy to stay. Volunteers were identified if you saw them when you were out walking, as they would cover their nose with a handkerchief as soon as they saw you and kept away from you – a similar approach to dealing with the current Coronavirus (although with less serious consequences if you came across one!). When we stayed, there was a pavement as a boundary that you couldn't cross. They found that even if you had the virus poured into your

---

* When the wind blew hard, it was incredibly noisy and you would hear it howling across the telephone wires.

nose, you only had a four in ten chance of actually getting a cold because there are so many different viruses, you would likely be immune to some of them. They studied all manner of treatments and situations: for example; volunteers were kept in wet, cold conditions, to see if that alone would give you a cold. One of the most interesting set of observations came from an experiment in which young children had been selected from five village schools in the Ebble Valley. Whenever a child developed a cold, they were taken to the unit to mix with the volunteers and as a reward given chocolates and cakes, in the expectation that the virus would be passed on to the volunteers. This was obviously popular with the children in the area and it was this type of experiment for which the unit was obviously very suitable. In the period from 1949 until it closed in 1987, 20,000 volunteers had passed through the unit. This is an extraordinarily long period for looking at how to deal with one disease from a research perspective.

The volunteers had to agree to the various rules and regulations that enabled these procedures to operate. Inevitably some volunteers did not fully conform exemplified by two young men in one hut who discovered that the ceiling panels were loose so they climbed into the roof space which enabled them to get into the female sections next door. Needless to say, this was not approved of and both parties were expelled!

Nature walks

Our children and those of our visitors, found it a fun place to be because it was a large open, safe place*. Unknown to us parents, my

---

* There was a large population of rabbits that often lived under our hut, which unfortunately if they died of myxomatosis, smelt horrible.

daughter and her friend would scavenge in the skips, possibly also containing medical waste, for bits of wood and other rubbish to make things. She still remembers one occasion of having to have a 'bleach bath' after one such escapade when found out.

Perhaps as a legacy from my own childhood in the country, not to mention my investigations with my microscope, I used to take groups of children from the local primary school on nature walks. One of my favourite spots to start was at the bottom of a chalk down where you could see water coming out of the ground as a spring, the beginning of a stream. The temperature never changed and even in the winter the water in the stream never froze. I believe it took seven years for the water to percolate through the chalk and it is chalk streams like this that provided the rivers which sustained constant crops of watercress.

The children who came on my country walks were encouraged by the teachers to write thank you letters, which usually said 'Dear Dr Butcher, thank you for taking us on a country walk." One rather sad letter said "Dear Dr Butcher, thank you for taking us on the walk. I asked my dad to take us but he said no" – a missed opportunity for a family to learn together about the natural world. On these various walks we occasionally saw March hares, a cuckoo in a nest, various raptors and small animals; possibly weasels, deer were common and a whole variety of birds, plants and flowers specific to the chalk downlands.

Being a fanatical gardener, I wanted to plant something in the space between our accommodation and the next hut. As it was a chalky area on the top of a down, anything one planted, had to be suitable for that kind of soil and I decided to grow some cabbages. Admittedly, they didn't grow quite as vigorously as I'd hoped, but the manager, Mr Thompson, was not impressed by my horticultural efforts and phoned my wife in a rather aggressive manner, suggesting cabbages were untidy. In fact, when reading about the history of the units a previous administrator wanted it to be self-sufficient in food and he was given the job of ploughing up the grass with a plough that didn't work properly. Mr Thompson was devoted to the work of the unit and perhaps for him it was more than just a job. But in the end, the cabbages had to go.

Asbestos: a curious episode

Soon after moving to the Common Cold Unit, I noticed that there was a fine white dust over much of our furniture. As this was the time when publications referring to asbestosis and cancer were often in medical journals, I thought that staff responsible for the unit would have considered the possibility of any hazard to human health due to the construction of these huts, although presumably no cases of cancer have been reported. Partly out of curiosity, but partly concern, I wrote to the director of the Cold Unit, but heard nothing in reply.

Sometime later, two men arrived with some apparatus to check on the air quality in the huts. We were asked to vacate the premises for a day and later I had a letter saying that they were safe to live in. That was all I heard. Many years later, I was told by a friend in the Medical Research Council that my letter had caused some panic in headquarters. Perhaps they thought I was going to write to the papers, but they didn't say anything to me at the time. It's interesting to reflect on the fact that this establishment was run by doctors who must have been sitting in the huts made of asbestos, reading the *Lancet* which had articles on asbestosis. It seems until I raised the matter no one previously mentioned it. However when I read through Mr Thompson's history of the unit, despite all the detail relating to the construction of the huts and day to day running of the place (including the daily menus), one word was not mentioned in the text: 'asbestos'.* I wondered if the white dust I saw could be broken into smaller dangerous particles when we used the hoover, though they did not test this when monitoring the air quality. Happily, we know of no one developing this disease and we left within 18 months. Years later, the huts were damaged in the 1987 gale and it closed down soon after and all research was stopped on the common cold and the area became a housing estate.

Health and safety: don't hold your breath

While I worked at Porton, the rules were that everybody in the building had to have a respirator to which you could attach chemical and or biological filters presumably as a safety measure in case of an accident. I managed to ignore this rule for about six months as I did not want to shave off my beard so that the mask fitted properly. However, they eventually said that if I didn't have the respirator fitted, they wouldn't let me in. The testing was done at CDE (Chemical Defence Establishment) where you put on the respirator with the appropriate filter and stepped in to a chamber, into which they would squirt some tear gas. I put on the respirator having shaved off my beard, but when they screwed on the filters, I stopped being able to breath. I was given "special dispensation" and grew back my beard, much to my daughter's (and everyone else's) relief!

---

* One is reminded of the 300 years it took the medical profession to link the occurrence of fevers with the presence of mosquitoes that to many ship owners and sailors who travelled to tropical regions was obvious.

The hole in the wall

In another incident relating to safety, it was discovered that one of the drains in my lab ran through the wall to the high containment area. Fortunately, I was on the 'clean side', but there should have been no connection at all. We found this out because after some time of being there, my lab gradually became warmer. When it was investigated, the workman who came first tried to give me their spanner to do the work. They were clearly nervous about coming into the lab. When they eventually summoned up the courage to come in and took the panels off the wall, one man looked in and said in his Wiltshire accent: "there's a big 'ole 'ere!". I left them to it.

Having escaped one biohazard, I managed to escape another which involved hepatitis B. Blood samples containing *Plasmodium falciparum* for my cultures were stored in liquid nitrogen in ampoules sent from my colleague Graham Mitchell in The Gambia. Unfortunately, on one occasion, I was in a hurry to get the work done and failed to wear the protective visor. The ampoule, supposedly a new safety type, exploded when taken out of the liquid nitrogen. There was a loud bang, (which I thought was a bomb), but my technician said, "you've got blood on your face". This must have been caused by a piece of the exploding plastic. I went to the medical staff on site, told them what had happened and filled in the appropriate form. The reaction of the cheery medic, when I told him it was human malaria, said that it was "very boring" – clearly expecting something like Ebola or some other deadly virus, which to him would have been more interesting. A year or two later, I was asked to oversee safety at the medical school in Newcastle, Australia – presuming because as I had worked at the MRE I was considered an 'expert' on laboratory safety. I decided to screen everybody as a start, including myself. I thereupon discovered I had a very high titre (concentration) of antibody to hepatitis B.

My guardian angel must've been hovering about somewhere, as I'd managed to vaccinate and thus protect myself from Hep B. I should have mentioned to the medic at Porton that the ampoule came from Africa and that other possible pathogens could have been present, though he probably should have enquired! Despite all the changes and legislation in relation to Health and Safety during the fifteen years since I had my first accident at the School of Hygiene, the change in personnel from a doorman to a medically qualified doctor, seemed to have made little difference.

Fostering in the early years

"It isn't who borns you what matters,
it's the ones who love you"

My wife Sue had qualified as a teacher but at an intellectual level she was always very interested in the development of babies and young children. One of her headmistresses told her she could rise to be a headmistress, so she must have had an innate talent with children. A colleague with whom she was having a discussion about child behaviour remarked on the fact that Sue had made an observation that was along the lines of the one of the experts of the time called Piaget, though she would never have read any of his books or papers. If it wasn't for the fact that she suffered frequently debilitating migraine throughout her life, maybe her career would have been different.

While I was at Guy's, we had planned to have another baby after our first two children, Michael and Helen. Around 1975 we then had another baby that was still-born, and possibly because of this we slipped into volunteering to look after young children in emergency fostering. We went through the process of applying to the local council and being interviewed in the usual way. However, what could have been a warning sign as to the way in which social services operated then was a rather surprising interview with one social worker. With our own children at about four or five, she tried to persuade us to adopt two children much older than ours – not just for an emergency but full-scale adoption. This was rather surprising to say the least but having firmly rejected this proposal we continued to go ahead with emergency fostering. During our time in New Malden, we had a couple of children, one toddler for about six months on and off and another primary school aged girl, who would come in only the clothes she stood up in (along with an army of nits in her long hair), and we would have to buy her clothes each time she stayed with us.

We continued fostering when we got to Salisbury once we had moved to our own house around 1979 – mostly babies or young children and with very different patterns of behaviour. One child, used to wake me up every morning by sitting on my head, with the smell of her nappy coming through the plastic pants. Her way of saying "time to get up!". Another, we took into our garden without shoes on, and when we put her down she screamed her head off – clearly not familiar with the feel of grass. Thankfully, eventually she got used to it.

On one occasion, we had a toddler and a baby who Sue used to carry as she was very tiny with no hair, whom we thought was only a few months old. When she put her down she crawled off and we realised she was older than she looked. She was probably malnourished, hence her size and lack of hair.

In Salisbury we were asked to look after two young boys during the week and at the weekends the father looked after them. These two lads were a continuous source of entertainment for all the time they were with us as their knowledge of the English language introduced us to some phrases we shall never forget.

We tried to feed them plain food that they would recognise, and feel happy with, but we could not always predict their preferences. For example, the younger one (we shall call him D), was given some peas and mashed potato with his meal. He looked at the peas, said in his strong Wiltshire accent "wha's tha'?", and Sue said "peas" so he smelt them, and said "I ain't 'eatin tha', tha' stinks!". We had a suspicion that their diet was somewhat restricted as every Friday evening when the dad came to collect them, all he produced was large bags of crisps and sweets and they seemed to only drink coke. On another occasion Sue had given them some sandwiches that D didn't seem to want to eat, possibly he was tired. Sue took the sandwich for herself, to which his response was "you stole my sandwich you bastard!"

When they wanted to attract your attention, they would say "cum 'er, cum 'er, cum 'er!" and grab hold of your legs. When the village policeman appeared at a fête one afternoon D not only grabbed my legs, but cowered behind me obviously very frightened, trying to stay out of sight. But we could never find out the cause of his fear. A phrase we should never forget from D when we took him to the toilet and asked 'have you finished' he'd say "yeah, the shits gone right back up me bum". At least clear and concise! His elder brother, was far quieter possibly because he couldn't get a word in edgeways with D about! When I took him into the garden on his own, he kept repeating the phrase "if D was here, he'd talk all the time".

We had a sloping front garden with a long driveway which D insisted on riding down on a bicycle but making no attempt to stop before he hit the garage banging his head at the bottom. On my second or third visit with this lad to casualty, I began to get some suspicious looks from the medical staff but had they seen D in action they would soon have seen the cause of the visits. D was very cross when his brother had a nose bleed that required a ride in an ambulance to hospital – I suspect he would have preferred this form of transport for his visits.

One Friday evening when their dad came to collect them he put them in his van which contained large cans of paint, specifically chosen by a well-off client. D managed to dislodge one of these, and expensive paint was soon covering the road. We did our best to scoop it up and put it back in the tin. Their dad was such a nice man he didn't reprimand him and just hoped nobody would notice. The last afternoon before they left us the Dad said to D, "was it alright?" And D gave us a thumbs up sign, for which we are forever grateful.

Of all the people we had to deal with, parents, children and social workers; the most difficult group were the social workers. When it came to emergency fostering, there was no special training and many had no experience of children, some not even having their own. We couldn't understand why on occasion, they would want to split up brothers and sisters regardless of the damage this would do. It was difficult to avoid the conclusion that everything they learnt was guided by a text book as one lady's answer always began with "the normal average baby". I wouldn't have thought any of the children we had to foster in an emergency would have been able to fit into this narrow view and that burden would only add to that of the foster parents. One would like to think that things have improved with the social care of children in today's society.

Moving Down Under

As my work at Porton Down was primarily centred around the *in vitro* conditions required to develop methods to culture malaria which had been achieved, it was time to move on. As the Australians were beginning a malaria programme it seemed it might be an interesting time to make a move in 1982.

Australia

Newcastle

I managed to get a small grant from the National Health and Medical Research Council to work on immunity to human malaria at Newcastle Medical School. We waited some time for visas to come through due to my son's heart murmur, meanwhile staying with very kind friends in a freezing cold vicarage over winter, for a few months as we had sold our house. We were not expecting such a long delay over a non-existent medical problem, but it gave the children a chance to have a last taste of winter in the English countryside.

Flight

After a 24 hour flight stopping at Bahrain and Singapore, we arrived in Australia in mid-summer to Sydney. Despite exhaustion and dehydration we managed to find the corner of the airfield for our transfer flight by Aero Pelican. We climbed aboard the De Haviland Otter but there was quite a delay, and I noticed while we were waiting, the pilot was reading comics. This did not inspire a great deal of confidence. While waiting for the pilot to finish his comic I remembered the story told by Frank Muir* of the early days of

---

* Frank Muir BBC

taking a plane to the Isle of Man before there were any pilots in uniform. One pilot, it was said, would come out of the cockpit with a ball of string which he gave to an old lady saying, "if the nose starts to go down, please pull on this string". His other activity was to sit amongst the passengers while they were waiting to take off, nearer the time he would start to complain about the delay saying if the pilot didn't come he would fly it himself, which at the appropriate time he then got up to sit in the pilot's seat. I have to confess, on our flight I sat waiting for the ball of string!

Thankfully, we finally landed safely in Newcastle without having to use the amply supplied sick bags and with a good view of the tops of the trees. We were taken to the Great Northern Hotel which hadn't seen a coat of a paint since the 1920's but was the only accommodation available. It had mysterious notices saying: "ties and no thongs" ('thongs' in Australia were the equivalent of flip-flops in the UK). Sue said unsurprisingly, she had a migraine and wanted to go home and the children were wide awake at 2:00 in the morning. Newcastle in the 80's was an old-fashioned Australian coal mining town, with BHP (Broken Hill Proprietary Company, a steel making plant), the main focus. The iron foundry spewed out pollution from the chimneys, which I could see from the red dots on my shirt when I went jogging one evening. It felt a long way from England.

Home by the sea

Our first home was Wirraway,* a block of flats for staff of the medical school. It also housed a large population of cockroaches of the species that didn't waste time laying eggs but produced its

---

* Now replaced by a 10-storey deluxe apartment block because of its prime location.

Newcastle harbour from our house on the hill

young fully formed, I believe the term is vivipary. At least we had a good view of the sea as we were right by the beach and could hear the waves gently crashing on the shore. It would have been a romantic scene if it wasn't for the cockroaches scratching about. We later moved to a traditional colonial terrace house on the hill, overlooking the port with a view of 20 miles. We could watch the coal ships waiting on the horizon – at one point during a strike there was a whole fleet of ships, each of 40,000 tons queuing out at sea. The crews, mostly from Japan, weren't allowed to come on land so they were under great stress on board and there was at least one murder that made the papers.

Papua New Guinea

Most of the work I had started was in conjunction with Ian Clark at the Australian National University in Canberra, but I did a trip to Papua New Guinea to collect blood samples. When I got to Port Moresby, the capital, I was told by some kind soul to run to make sure that I got a seat on the internal flight, otherwise the seats were all taken up by school children on the way home – it was their version of the school bus.

There is a central Highlands area of Papua New Guinea where the is no malaria, so when these people came down to the lowlands, they contracted the disease. This was characterised by a massively enlarged spleen (called hyper-reactive malarial splenomegaly). The great expert on this was an Australian doctor called Greg Crane who also provided me with a few serum samples. Normally when you get malaria the spleen enlarges (which is why the doctor will prod you in that area on examination). But as you become immune, the spleen returns to its normal size. In patients with HMS, the spleen remained enlarged or even 2-3 times normal size and could be fatal. HMS is specific to the highland people of Papua New Guinea.

I was allowed to go with the technicians who were collecting blood for the blood bank from the villagers near Madang, a highly malarial area. I spent an afternoon in a hospital making blood films to diagnose malaria, usually from babies. This involved stabbing a tiny finger with a hypodermic needle, but I was much too diffident and the technician with me said I was too soft and took over. Not surprisingly, they cried as soon as they saw a man in a white coat – unless they were very ill and then they were too lethargic. When I went out with the blood van I unwisely sat behind the driver and since everybody

Papua New Guinea near Madang

chewed the beetle nut, and spat out the remains, I was lucky not to return home with a shirt covered in blood and beetle juice.

Because all the blood collected in Papua New Guinea came from people exposed to malaria and probably immune, to help with their work I had told them I would arrange for some normal non-immune Australian blood to be sent to them in Madang. So, I packed up a few containers to be collected by Qantas after I'd returned from Papua New Guinea. The following Sunday I had a phone call from someone in Sydney airport asking me if I had an export licence to send blood abroad. I said I had no such licence and had not been told I needed one. The phone rang again and I was asked if I knew where on the plane the blood had been put in the cargo area; somehow they thought I'd personally placed it there. I then pointed out that there were 300 people on the plane who all had blood that they were taking with them out of Australia, again probably without export licences. Anyway, in the finish (as my aunt Kit would say), the much-needed blood arrived in Madang, leaving me with the feeling that Australian bureaucracy is almost worse than ours.

G'day

Outside of work, we made some good friends and as everyone knows, the Australians are a very convivial group of people. During our time in Newcastle and being near the Hunter Valley, I was invited to go walking with a friend in the rainforest. Before we left, Kerry advised me to wear sturdy boots as leeches were common. The leeches inject an anaesthetic in their saliva so you don't notice them and then an anticoagulant so the blood keeps flowing. While we were walking, I didn't notice anything unusual but when we got home my boots were full of blood; obviously my boots were not sturdy enough. It put my daughter off ever walking in rain forests.

As a family, we decided to try camping once in the bush, travelling down what was meant to be a main road, but was in fact a dirt track. We stayed overnight by a stream and there was a hut nearby with some poles that proved alarming when, during the storm that arrived that night, they were struck by lightning. Sue was convinced it struck the tent, but there were no burn marks, so it must have missed us. Needless to say, we spent the next night in the car. Apart from a snake in the stream when Michael went swimming there were no other incidents. The striking colours of the birds in the bush were some compensation for the inconveniences we suffered. We are obviously not the camping types – being feeble cabbages!

To Canberra and more immunology

The work situation became very difficult in Newcastle and I only discovered later that I was not welcome by some people even before I had arrived. The head of department was the only person with whom I did not get on well with in all my 40 years of research. So we moved to Canberra at the end of my 3-year grant to continue work with Ian Clark and colleagues.

As already mentioned, the focus on immunity to malaria at Guy's was on antibodies and therefore specific to the parasite species involved. So, once you become immune to one species of *Plasmodium* you are not immune to any other. However, Ian's work on mice and our work on monkeys immunised with merozoites and FCA* had shown that immunity at the beginning of infection was not specific and was characterised by the presence of damaged parasites within the red cell – the crisis forms first described by the Taliaferro's.[†] This was shown particularly clearly by electron microscopy by Lawrie

---

* Freund's Complete Adjuvant
† Taliaferro, WH and Taliaferro, L G (1929)

Bannister. This raised the question of what was causing the damage to the parasite that was normally protected by the red cell membrane. Our work in Canberra was to determine what was causing this damage. The other part of the story was that the control of the rodent parasite was the result of the over activation of the immune system that also caused the illness.

Part of my contribution was culturing human malaria in the presence of the products of the white cells, in particular, macrophages that cause the parasite damage. Macrophages are a type of white cell derived from monocytes (see photograph 25) which are present in the blood, along with five other types of white cell. At the Tunbridge Wells conference I went to in 1966, (mentioned earlier), when Dr Humphrey in his lecture said "we don't really know what lymphocytes do", by the time I went to Canberra, it was known that lymphocytes were a major part of the immune system. All the white cells "talk to each other" by secreting various biological chemical signals. In the photograph, there is a macrophage surrounded by infected red cells and some uninfected ones. These are "stuck" to the macrophage by the presence of antibody and a bridge between the parasitised red cells and the macrophage.* At the same time, the macrophage has secreted

---

* In George Bernard Shaw's play The Doctor's Dilemma (1907) there is an amusing exchange that explains the activity of macrophages and antibodies: "Sir Patrick: Opsonin? What the devil is opsonin?

Ridgeon: Opsonin is what you butter the disease gems with to make your white blood corpuscles eat them.

Sir Patrick: That's not new. I've heard this notion that the white corpuscles – what is it that what's his name? – Metchnikoff – calls them?

Ridgeon: Phagocytes.

Sir Patrick: Aye, phagocytes: yes, yes, yes, Well, I heard this theory that the phagocytes eat up the disease germs years ago: long before you came into fashion. Besides, they don't always eat them.

Ridgeon: They do when you butter them with opsonin. " from Living with Germs. p.79

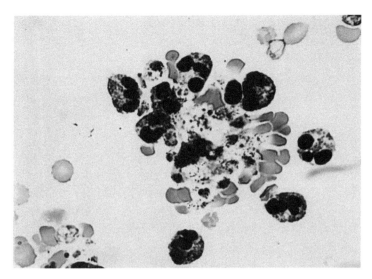

Macrophage phagocytosing infected cells and PMN being attracted to the action

one or more of the biological signals into the medium. This signal is attracting another type of white cell, PMN (Polymorphonuclear cell) to the scene of action. In simple terms, this is how the immune system protects us from bugs. When I retired there were nearly 20 different biological signals (interleukins). The most important of which is called Tumour Necrosis factor (TNF)*. This is a major player in the control of infection, but is also very important when over produced as it causes all the symptoms that we recognise when we are ill, especially high fevers typical of malaria.

---

* TNF was discovered by two different groups working independently. The group working in Africa identified a peptide that caused weight loss in cattle and called it cachectin. An American group identified the same molecule in studies on macrophages, but as it killed some strains of cancer they called it 'Tumour Necrosis Factor'. Its main function is nothing to do with cancer and more recently it has been found in all living organisms.

As the parasites were not damaged by antibody the question arises as to what was killing them. Most people now have heard of free radicals and the damage could result from these or a number of other agents. Most important of these is the free radical; a form of oxygen that causes oxidated damage. This is what causes butter to go rancid and tyres to deteriorate. If you look at the ingredients of certain foods, they will contain things like vitamin E and vitamin C and sodium sorbate to inhibit the oxidative damage.* Macrophages release other chemicals (probably proteins) that also cause the abnormalities we see in Lawrie Bannisters electron microscopy. It is when these functions of macrophages and other types of white cells are out of control, that the tissues of the host are also damaged. This is probably what occurs in autoimmune conditions such as rheumatoid arthritis, SLE (systemic lupus erythematosus), including neurodegenerative diseases.

Malaria and other conditions

HIV

At about this time, HIV[†] appeared in which the virus destroyed the lymphocytes (the cells that constitute a large part of the immune system). If you deplete mice of the lymphocytes and then give them malaria, they cannot control the infection and the malaria multiplies rapidly and the mice die with nearly all their red cells infected. I would have expected humans with HIV to follow a similar pattern, but initially the early papers seemed to show that HIV had only a mild effect in the presence of malaria.

---

* This is explained clearly in a book "*Free Radicals in Biology & Medicine*" Barry Halliwell & John M C Gutteridge.

† Human Immunodeficiency virus

Subsequently it was shown that people did get worse with malaria but still not to the same degree as mice although it could have been that people were dying of other infections before the malaria took hold. I wrote a couple of reviews on this aspect, hoping to stimulate some discussion.

Autoimmune disease

In 1970, Dr Brian Greenwood (now Professor Sir Brian Greenwood), observed that in West African hospitals there were fewer cases of autoimmune disease, such as rheumatoid arthritis and lupus (systemic lupus erythematosus). Malaria is known to suppress the immune system and Greenwood and colleagues did a few experiments on mice but the subject has not been given any significant attention. On reading about this topic, I learnt that people of West Africa descent tend to have higher rates of these diseases than white people when they become resident in Europe or America. This suggests that malaria may have selected for genes that can give some protection for malaria in Africa, but at the same time render the carriers more vulnerable to autoimmune disease when they live in Europe or America. A major player of the immune system is the group of cells known as macrophages responsible for defending us against bacteria and other infections. But these are also important in causing the damage of tissues that occurs in autoimmune disease.

The conditions I was interested in, in addition to rheumatoid and lupus, were sarcoidosis (an uncommon lung disease) and granulomatosis. Both are very uncommon in African and European populations which makes it more difficult to detect significant differences between various groups, but there is also evidence for macrophage involvement in the diseases.

To my mind any source of information such as the interaction with malaria could perhaps be useful in understanding how the body reacts to these diseases. It is only recently that immunologists seem to have taken an interest in these interactions.

Publication: 'Traveller's Guide'

While I was at the ANU there were anthropology students going off to do field studies in tropical regions of South East Asia. Drug resistance by malaria to the tablets taken as prophylactics was becoming more common. The students became rather frustrated with the medics as sometimes, although they were declared parasite negative, they continued to be ill. One young man who had some connection with Japanese royalty died of cerebral malaria. Although it was not official, to cope with the increasing levels of frustrated students, as we had the time and experience, we could look at blood films for longer periods so the hospital would send samples to us to detect any parasites present. Towards the end of my time, I would give brief lectures to groups of students on malaria and I wrote a small volume "*An Intelligent Traveller's Guide to Malaria*" so they would have something to refer to. We only published a limited number of copies and most of those went to charities working in the tropics, who found the guide helpful.

Living in Canberra

Canberra, when we were there in the 80's, was remarkably small for a capital city. Nearly all the people who worked there (around 70,000) were civil servants. The major highway was between Sydney in New South Wales and Melbourne in Victoria. The road to Canberra, was off this road, was not even fully tarmacked at the time. The train service was so poor and infrequent, taxi drivers didn't even know where the station was. There was a small airport outside Canberra,

Malaria; The Intelligent Traveller's Guide book

but most visitors came by car. Friends who came to visit would overshoot the turn off to Canberra and end up in Queenbeyan, another town just outside Canberra. Today, with the new Parliament House having been built, I'm sure that it is now more connected!

Excursions: Coober Pedy and Tasmania

One of the most interesting places in Australia that we had the opportunity to visit, was Coober Pedy, which is some five hundred miles north of Adelaide and known for its mining of opal. We travelled there by an overnight coach from Adelaide. They would say, if you were taking a photo of something not to step back in case you fell into one of the miners' holes – in fact the name Coober Pedy is from the Aboriginal Kupa-Piti – meaning "white fellas' hole". Everything there is underground – including the hotel because it is so hot and dry. If you have a house and you needed another room - you could just dig another room out of the rock. The only problem was that if people who did the digging found black opal, they'd take it with them and keep digging and the owners would return to a bigger hole than expected. We visited an underground chapel and cinema, all the spaces underground kept at a cool and pleasant atmosphere. It was said that there were 48 different nationalities who worked there. All supplies, including food and water, are brought in by lorry or train.

The underlying rock is gypsum, which is fairly soft. The miners would use explosives to make big enough holes in which to look for the brown seams in the gypsum for the opal, digging it out with a pick axe. The Australian miners had a rather casual attitude to explosives as there was a notice at the entrance to the cinema that requested that 'explosives not to be brought inside'! Occasionally they would find opalised fish – opal has a highwater-content and the minerals are what give it the colour. Black opal is the most expensive and sought after. On a Saturday night, they would take their findings to the Chinese dealers in the hotel.

Uluru

We took a separate trip to Uluru. What struck me about this trip was that it had rained and the desert was in flower, which was a sight to see. Internal flights were expensive then and so most of our travelling was done by coach, stopping overnight in Adelaide to see friends and then another coach to Alice Springs through the night. They were vast distances.

Tasmania

We took our car on a ferry to Tasmania across the Bass Strait which is a notoriously rough stretch of water. We travelled all the way round Tasmania where it rained almost all the time. It was very heavily forested with many streams and much like Wales and seemed slightly out of time by about 50 years – including the decor. The most interesting place was Queenstown with a museum of geology which was incredibly extensive, like the Natural History Museum in South Kensington.

They had been mining copper there for many years, and smelting it which killed off a lot of the trees. You could see the water in the streams was green from the copper deposits. It degraded and made the local area very barren. When they decided to stop doing the mining and smelting, the trees began to grow back, and there was a quandary about whether to let it grow back or leave it as a tourist attraction.

Back to Blighty

"You can take the boy out of London,
but you can't take London out of the boy"

My studies on *P. falciparum in vitro* to which we added serum from PNG from people who were immune was coming to an end. One relaxing afternoon, I was reading the *New Scientist* and came across an article about a strain of mouse with virtually no immune system (Severe Combined immunodeficiency; SCID mice), alongside an article about children with no immunity, who had to live in 'bubbles'. I discovered that there was a group in the ANU who used these mice to study diabetes by implanting Langerhans (the cells that produce insulin) under the kidney capsule. It occurred to me that if you could do this with human liver cells you would potentially have a culture system for testing drugs and vaccines. Researchers who cultured the human liver cells using traditional methods were not very successful – partly because the salivary glands of a mosquito were always contaminated by bacteria. At that time, we were not allowed to infect mosquitoes with human malaria in Australia as they had eradicated it. So, I wrote to Bob Sinden at Imperial College in London, because his group worked on mosquitoes and the interesting liver stages and had an insectary, whereby we eventually got a grant to set up the SCID mouse/mosquito/liver cell culture system. This prompted our return to England. With my daughter already back in the UK and settled, we left our house in the dubious hands of our son to finish the sale, while he finished his degree course at the ANU.

Back to UK

Imperial College

Once back in the UK at Imperial College, we contacted the nearest medical school and asked if they would be able to supply us with very small amounts of human liver. I learnt how to expose the kidney in a SCID mouse and insert a small amount of tissue. Obviously everything had to be done under sterile conditions as it would only take a few bacteria to infect the mouse. Naturally, mosquitoes are covered in bacteria but after having dissected out the salivary glands these were washed several times by centrifugation then injected into a vein in the mouse. I rather enjoyed this micro surgery which reminded me of my early days at college 'operating' on amoebae.

Our hope was to see if after a few days the kidney from the mouse could be fixed and sectioned to see if there were any liver stage schizonts. Unfortunately, despite their promises to supply us with very tiny amounts of liver tissue the doctors we had contacted lost any interest they might have had in this project and we were never able to put any adult human liver cells into the mice, which was very frustrating. This wasn't the first time I had been promised materials to help with a project and the other party failed to play their part. I realise now that I should have made a greater effort to get to know the doctors concerned so that they would feel it was to their advantage to be involved.

Although we didn't achieve our primary objective, the mice proved useful to several other groups and we were able to publish a number of papers. An American group attempted the same goal using the same methodology, but although they published what they claimed were photographs of liver schizonts, we were not convinced that it was the genuine article.

Imperial mosquitoes

Most of the work at Imperial was concerned with various aspects of the biology of the mosquito and the transmission of malaria but with a major emphasis on developing a transmission blocking vaccine. Such a vaccine would be unconventional as the people immunised would not receive any personal protection. However, the community as a whole would be protected by any antibodies present in the blood of the people immunised and therefore picked up by the mosquito population. Experimentally it had been shown that antibodies to mosquitoes and to the sexual stages of the parasite was easily achieved and that transmission could be inhibited.

Maintaining the mosquito colony was labour intensive as the conditions required for transmitting the malaria had to be just right, and all of the group, including Bob, were involved. About 10000 mosquitoes a week were needed to maintain the colony and to do experiments. Some of the time we would have enough money to pay a full-time technician, but otherwise we worked out a rota between us. For those unfamiliar with breeding mosquitoes, one obviously has to start with eggs which were put into bowls of water containing a few minerals. The eggs developed into larvae that fed on a fish diet and these in turn developed into pupae. The pupae were removed using a gentle suction and put into dishes placed in net cages in which they became adults. These were fed a sugar solution equivalent to

Female Anopheles stephensi feeding on volunteer. Photo: Bob Sinden

plant nectar. Others would feed on an anaesthetised rat, to maintain the colony, as without a blood feed the females would not produce eggs. Obviously all this has to be done under high containment conditions especially when it comes to infecting mosquitoes with human malaria in vaccine trials.

Through studying the mosquitoes we were interested in finding out what stimulated the male gametocytes to suddenly produce the microgametes. If you didn't choose the right time to put them with the females then you would not get any infection in the mosquito. The microgametocytes were triggered by a number of different factors; such as a drop in temperature from 37°C; the pH. and a chemical produced by the mosquito. In contrast to the other parasite species, the gametocytes of *P. falciparum* took a long time to develop in culture – about three weeks. The only way of observing the state of the gametocytes was to look for the ex-flagellating males under the microscope.

Mosquitoes and chloroquine

A potentially very important aspect on which we only did preliminary experiments with a group in Denmark, was to find evidence for possible interactions of a common anti-malarial (chloroquine) and the parasites in the mosquito gut. The people in Denmark studied a human population in Africa and found that if patients who had taken chloroquine were then bitten by mosquitoes, the transmission of malaria was enhanced. I did some work with a student and we found evidence suggesting that the immune system of the mosquito was suppressed by chloroquine (immunosuppressive in humans) and therefore more of the malarial parasites survived, thus increasing transmission of the malaria. Unfortunately, we could not take this work any further at that time.

Oxford vaccine

Although most of the work was studying rodent malaria transmission, we also provided mosquitoes for the Oxford group who were also attempting to devise an effective malaria vaccine. As with our work on developing a vaccine to merozoites at Guy's the Oxford group in contrast, were attempting to develop a vaccine based on sporozoites. This research involved groups of 20 volunteers, usually five controls and the others being given different types of potential malaria vaccines. The method of testing the vaccine was to expose volunteers to the bites of up to five infected mosquitoes. The volunteers were then monitored by taking blood samples over the course of the next two weeks by which time all the volunteers who were controls (usually 5) would have parasites in the blood but were cured with chloroquine. The other volunteers would have had three different types of trial vaccine so that if they were not immune they would become blood positive.

Writing about this aspect of malaria reminded me that back at the 1974 WHO meeting to sort out priorities in malaria research including the possibility of a vaccine. I presented our work on *P. knowlesi* merozoites that protected rhesus monkeys when injected into a muscle. All of the monkeys treated in this way were rendered immune.

A completely different approach by a group headed by Dr Ruth Nussenzweig in New York was based on treating mosquitoes which had sporozoites in the salivary glands. It had been known for many years that X-ray, heat treatment and other physical applications applied to the mosquito if done at the correct dosage, would leave the sporozoites in the salivary glands able to invade the liver cells but to develop no further. This meant that it was possible to develop a vaccine based on sporozoites as opposed to merozoites. Because our work seemed at the time to be making more progress than the New York group, a representative of WHO said at the end of the meeting, that we should recommend everybody working in this field to concentrate on merozoites. At this point Ruth looked somewhat in a state of shock but nobody said anything. I was the youngest and least experienced researcher there, but I took the WHO man to task that his remarks were ill advised and showed a lack of understanding of how science works. I pointed out that his approach was that of a bureaucrat and not a scientist. No one else said anything but afterwards Sydney agreed with me.

What is curious about this story is that the recent Oxford vaccine that is proving successful is based on sporozoites. Unfortunately, vaccines based on merozoites, as far as I know at present have not been successful. As it happened, at my last days at Imperial, I was involved in testing the Oxford vaccine based on sporozoites – having defended the "opposition" in 1974, I joined them at the end of my time at Imperial.

Tomorrow's World

Towards the end of my time at Imperial, we had a visit from the *Tomorrow's World* team from the BBC. It was a popular programme that presented short but up to date news in science and technology. In the last edition of that programme they came to enquire about the work we were doing in Bob Sinden's group on the possibility of developing a vaccine that would stop the transmission of malaria by mosquitoes. The presenter who was an experienced journalist interviewed Bob in a sort of lurid blue light in the insectary that made it look more dramatic and I was asked to wear my lab coat, and look as though I was talking about the science to another man, also in a lab coat, who had only just arrived in the department from Italy. We didn't know what to say to each other – all I could think of was "what's the Italian for rhubarb?"! So we had to stare at each other pretending to talk while being filmed. Having finished her interview with Bob, I noticed she was walking up and down the lab saying to herself "chloroquine and paludrine, chloroquine and paludrine, chloroquine and pal..", obviously worried that she was going to get it wrong. My other contribution was squeezing a hypodermic needle full of water under the blue light looking as though I was going to inject a vaccine into somebody and later putting my hand into a cage of mosquitoes with the females filling up with my blood. Somewhere we have in the family heirlooms a copy of the tape. It was a whole morning of filming to produce two minutes of chat – an interesting insight into the workings of TV.

Working with animals

It seems appropriate at this point to put down something on the subject of working with animals. Although, work involving experiments on animals is controversial, when this is put in context with the vast numbers of people suffering from malaria (one child dies every two minutes) the number of animals used compared to the fatality rate of the disease, was minimal. Any suffering involved in our experiments was kept to an absolute minimum as we had to conform to the regulations outlined by an Act of Parliament. Although this act was passed in 1876 the general principles inherent in the act still apply in a revised act of 1986, which is much more detailed than the original.* The conditions under which monkeys are kept, now in colonies as opposed to individual cages, are carefully regulated, such that anyone breaking the law can be prosecuted.

One experience early on in my career was when one of the lecturers in anatomy at Guy's, had heard that we worked on monkeys and wanted a monkey, to prepare a skeleton. We arranged a time for the monkey to be handed over to him after the end of my experiment, but when he arrived in the lab he said he had a problem. I said "what's that?" He explained "I'm a Buddhist I can't kill anything" I was tempted to say, "well I'm a good Christian I'll kill it for you", which I then did by a lethal dose of anaesthetic, and off he went with his dead monkey. This was the first time I'd come across this philosophical approach, potentially hindering research. However, I have noticed over the

_____

* I wrote various articles for the Research Defence Society, which is now an advocacy group: Understanding Animal Research. A video was made in 1992 with R Scouse to explain the use of marmosets in Parkinson's Disease.

years an increasing number of people wanting to do a PhD that has to involve experiments on mice. It then transpires that when they come to the practical issue of infecting and bleeding the mice they decide that they can't actually do the work but get someone else to do the work for them. I don't think this is an acceptable approach to research.

English malaria

In addition to malaria, my other obsession for many years has been history and I was pleased when a history journal – *History Today* – published an article I wrote to celebrate the 100 years since Ross discovered the transmission of malaria by mosquito. There is plenty of evidence that malaria – the agues – was a health hazard in this country until the late 1800's, the last outbreak being in 1917. It was mostly around the estuaries of rivers along the eastern/south eastern coasts as the transmitting mosquitoes preferred brackish water in which to lay their eggs. Although there was good documentary clinical evidence of people suffering from the agues, no one as far as I could determine, had attempted to identify the precise species, so this seemed to be a useful project to pursue. Coincidentally I came into contact with an historian from the Wellcome Collection, who had been collating data on the health of the clergy in the malarial areas from the Bishop's visitations in the 17-19th Centuries.

Some vicars were so affected by the agues that to reduce the suffering of their families they moved to less hazardous areas and left their curates (presumably mostly unmarried) to look after their parishes. In addition to this information, Daniel Defoe in his *Tour around England* reported that many of the men in these costal counties married girls from inland who had not been exposed to the agues and therefore had a higher mortality. Many men claimed to have had several wives as a result – one told Defoe he had been married to fourteen wives, though Defoe thought he had "fibbed a little".

The plan that we devised was using the clinical data linked to known clergy buried in churches and to exhume the bones and look for evidence of malarial infection – probably DNA, but possibly proteins and malarial pigment. We were ready to begin when the C of E archaeologist told us that in Victorian times there was a shortage of burial space which meant that most remans had been removed from the tombs and piled up in crypts. Consequently, we would be unable to identify the bones and correlate them with our known clergymen. So another addition to the "Book of Heroic Failures". Perhaps one day someone will have another go at this project.

Extracurricular activities

In the House of Commons, MP's may form informal Parliamentary committees on any subject which attracts their attention or any problem that needs to be discussed. Speakers with particular experience are invited and the meetings are open to the public. Malaria was one subject that attracted a small number of MPs and Bob was invited to speak but passed on the invitation to me while I was still at Imperial. Every now and again we would have a bigger meeting with a panel of people experienced in one of the different aspects within malaria. This was especially important in consideration of matters such as overseas aid, drug resistance, mosquito resistance to insecticides and so forth. These were useful meetings and I did feel that they were appreciated for the forum in which to have an exchange of ideas., it was a good opportunity for MPs to get up to date information and when I was no longer able to attend I received a thank you letter for my contribution, such as it was.

Retirement: time to waffle

It was in 1999, during a lecture I was giving to a research group at Imperial that I noticed one of my fingers shaking. After various other incidences of this symptom, I realised it was Parkinson's and was later diagnosed. Due to this condition not being very conducive to dissecting mosquitoes with fine needles under the microscope, I gradually wound down my work at imperial. I continued to play a part in an honorary position, attending research meetings and keeping in touch with colleagues.

Malaria Consortium

It was at one of these Parliamentary meetings that I was introduced to Pat Scutt, one of the founders of what eventually became the Malaria Consortium. This is a very large charity concerned with tropical diseases, but mainly malaria. Pat persuaded me to became a trustee and so through this I met many of the people actively trying to control malaria – in some areas succeeding with the use of insecticide treated bed nets and appropriate drugs. The Technical Director was Dr Sylvia Meek, who was very dedicated and was a great loss when she sadly died of cancer. As someone with experience of malaria I was able to ask appropriate questions, particularly with regard to drugs, resistance and general technical problems, to help in any way I could by way of up to date information. At a meeting they held in Uganda to see the staff on the ground, I was very impressed by their hard work and dedication, which continues to this day.

Parkinson's and TNF

I also became involved with the Parkinson's Disease Society and sat on one of their committees to do with communicating to the

Celebrating 25 years of malaria research

public and raising awareness of the disease. I went to many research talks and on several occasions to the annual general meeting to hear the latest ideas for treating the disease and research findings. However, in none of the lectures I attended or in the literature that was sent out did I read the words Tumour Necrosis Factor (TNF). Considering the importance of this molecule and associated signals and the rapidly rising publications, I felt the focus was too narrow and though I raised the topic myself at every opportunity through meetings and letters I made little progress. Although the chairman did seem to be receptive to the TNF story as she was also involved in a charity concerning rheumatoid arthritis, I became too frustrated to continue and combined with the state of my own health and my wife's health, it became too difficult to continue.

Kew: berries not for eating

Another activity I became involved in was doing a morning a week at the Royal Botanic Gardens in Kew and when I started I was expecting to be given a trowel to do some weeding. But instead, I found myself in front of a computer doing searches on databases, looking at plants that are good for you and not so good for you. Having in mind that different parts of a plant have different properties and may therefore have various uses. I spent one session in the garden asking people to fill in a card as to what plants their grandmothers might have used as food or medicines. Most of the answers were common things, like dandelions* and nettles but occasionally one would come across an unusual treatment. One story I remember was the use of spiders webs collected to form a sort of pad that could be placed over a cut reportedly helping

---

* Dandelion and burdock as a drink was a common example.

it to heal. This would not be surprising as spiders webs contain antifungal and antibacterial properties*. All this information went towards the production of a book on poisonous plants for use by people looking after young children; this saved a member of staff having to answer the phone first thing every morning from a worried parent or child minder about one of their children having consumed a few berries. One of my greatest pleasures at Kew was cycling through the gardens on sunny frosty mornings before the public arrived – and not being shouted at by a park keeper!

Communicating science

When I first started on malaria in the 1960's it was hardly ever mentioned in newspapers or in the media generally. If I told people I was working on this disease, they would look at me blankly and say why don't you do something useful, like working on the common cold. Even GPs seemed to be unaware that if their patients were going abroad they would need antimalarial tablets and I know of one GP whose son went to Nigeria without any medication because his father had said there was no more malaria in Nigeria. The colonial era had come to an end and so only the people who had served in the tropics were aware of the problem. It wasn't until people started to go to tropical and sub-tropical countries for holidays and some of them became ill and even a few died, soon after their return that the media started to report it. After they returned home and got sick, the doctor would often diagnose flu. The fact that malaria was one of the biggest killers in the human population seemed to have escaped most people as they assumed that DDT† had killed off most

---

* I later read that they were doing some research on this at Texas University.

† Dichlorodiphenyltrichloroethane a pesticide

of the mosquitoes. Some anti-malaria drugs had side effects that caused problems in a few cases. Unfortunately, these were picked up by the media who gave the impression that they were actually more dangerous than the malaria, which of course was not true.

As a pupil at Emanuel a young PhD student who was working on bees came to give us a talk after school and remembering this I decided I would follow his example. However, because malaria was so unknown, I would not be invited by whoever ran after school science clubs unless I invited myself. While I was at Guy's, I wrote to the head teacher at Nonsuch School in Surrey, partly because I thought it would be a good way to recruit technical staff. In fact, my first technician came from Nonsuch and I asked her when she had been with us a few months if it was my talk that encouraged her to apply for the post and she replied "no, I didn't understand a word". I think she was trying to deflate my ego! Nevertheless, I took every opportunity I could to tell people about the huge numbers of people in Africa, Asia and South America who lost children to this disease and which is largely uncontrolled, even today. As always I offered to give these talks without any charge and visited schools, both independent and state funded, as well as University of the Third Age (U3A), history groups, primary and secondary schools.

I have no idea how many people I might have talked to, having done this throughout my career, assuming perhaps it could have been a thousand or more I can only remember two occasions when the use of animals in research was questioned. This suggests to me that when people understand the nature of the problem they accept the need for some animal experimentation. This confirmed my belief that continuing to give these talks was very worthwhile.

Another reason for continuing along this path was that it helped people with no understanding of biology or of science and therefore would never even consider a career in science. Furthermore, since most scientists are funded by government and charities, we have an obligation to tell them what we are doing.

Whenever I have visited a lab and talked to PhD students I have asked them what they do and usually why are they researching their particular speciality and how they go about it. Quite often it is proved difficult, even for someone like me with a scientific background, to get clear answers particularly in relation to the question "why". Very often people become so immersed in the detail of their research and the technological advances that they have made, that they seem to have forgotten why they began the work in the first place. One would expect that (with the exception of highly mathematical subjects), most people in biomedical research for example, should be able to summarise their work in terms understandable by a layman. After all this is usually necessary in the process of applying for funding. Somewhere I read a quotation, I think from a young girl who said: "how do I know what I think, until I hear what I say?". I suggest this is a useful phrase for every PhD student on which to ponder.

I enjoyed giving these talks enormously, although I may be a bit nervous to begin with as one can never be sure if one's audience are going to understand what I'm talking about. However, I have had some interesting responses: after one lecture to a group of well to do more 'mature' ladies in Kensington, I was told they fully expected to be bored but instead were fascinated. I am glad to say this has been the most common reaction; even from children or young people who could have found the science challenging, it didn't seem to be a problem. One single factor which has always helped the talk to go smoothly and distract any potentially difficult behaviour was because I always took with me some pots of live mosquitoes which I usually produced as the last thing. This always provoked more interest in those who might have been getting bored especially when I put my hand on the netting and allowed the mosquitoes to bite.

Every year, in this country, we have a science week and along with colleagues from Imperial colleague and Oxford I have helped in these demonstrations at the Royal Society. One of my colleagues, medically qualified and specialising in malaria research, told me after one of these demonstrations, that his father was a taxi driver and that I was the only person who had ever managed to explain malaria to him which left me feeling my efforts were worthwhile. One year I organised an exhibit in a shopping mall in Crawley with a group of sixth form students from a local grammar school. Apart from the usual photographs, we had pieces of the Cinchona tree from Kew Gardens the bark of which contained quinine. Again, we had cages of live mosquitoes. One of the girls was so enthusiastic she would rush up to people loaded down with shopping and say "do you want to put your hand in my mosquitoes?". This did not always produce the positive response she hoped for.

Sixth formers in Crawley shopping mall with malaria exhibit in science week.

The Big Questions

"I Think there's something in it."

According to one psychiatrist, it is about the age of 14 that boys seem to develop a kind of moral code that they tend to cling to most of their lives. I seem to have followed that sort of a pattern, becoming a Christian round about 14 and that helped me to have a purpose, although I still had the problems of communication with my parents and anxieties and difficulties in relationships at school. As far as I can remember, often there were occasions if I passed someone in a corridor and they would say to me 'cheer up Geoff' presumably because I looked depressed I suppose. As I learnt more about biology and evolution from A level until university, I found it very difficult to hold on to any faith. Part of the trouble was that I wanted my view of the world through both a scientific and spiritual to be consistent. I seemed to have forgotten over the decades greater minds than mine had struggled with these problems and not got very far. One day, as a student, I was coming out of the Natural History Museum where I had been using the library and I crossed over Cromwell Road. I was looking into the bookshop that sold second hand and remainder books and I saw a small painting of a virgin and child and suddenly, out the blue came a flash of light I can only explain as a sensation of hope that lifted me out of depression. It was quite strange; it had never happened to me before and never again and I can't remember how long the effect lasted. It somehow didn't solve all the problems and I went on searching, looking for evidence of the existence of God and all that sort of thing. I even spent one afternoon in Fulham library reading through the English translation of the Quran and was surprised to find it had verses from the Old Testament. Gradually, as time went by, going to Bristol to do the PGCE, I remember thinking that biology can explain everything. I recall being almost told off by another Christian student that that wasn't the way to go. Somehow going to Nigeria, I started worrying less about these sorts of problems and decided that the importance of being a Christian was doing something useful – John Wesley's rule for life came to mind:

> "Do all the good you can,
> By all the means you can,
> In all the ways you can
> In all the places you can
> At all the times you can.
> To all the people you can,
> As long as you can."

I heard on television some sixth form children being questioned on their knowledge of English history. Sadly, they were unaware of the battle of Waterloo, let alone other great events in our history and one can be quite sure that they would not have heard of the Clapham sect.* We owe a great deal to ordinary Christian people who campaigned against the evils of their day, everything from child labour in mines and factories to the treatment of criminals. Despite my doubts and fears about Christian truth I am attracted by the behaviour and strength of faith of my fellow Christians. Most people would not admit to praying or going to church but as a last resort when things go badly wrong they often turn to prayer and the church. Even though people may not openly admit to the fact that they pray, as Sir Alistair Hardy has demonstrated in his book "*the Spiritual Nature of Man*", some form of "spiritual experience" is not

---

* Notable figures included William Wilberforce and were concerned with social activism.

The picture that gave hope: Madonnina: Ferruzzi (1853-1934),
Photo courtesy of Wimbledon Fine Art Ltd

uncommon. Such experiences are not always pleasant and people may have a sense of evil which is almost tangible. It is in thinking along these lines that I am inclined to agree with Mr Hislop (of *Have I got News for You* fame), that "I think there's something in it".

Reflections on Research

The recent pandemic caused by Corona virus has stimulated an almost dramatic explosion of information and confusion in the interaction of science and the media. The reputable presenters of news in all the various formats have no doubt done their best to provide accurate information in a rapidly changing situation. However, the democratic tradition that we fortunately have in this country results in equal time being allowed to any collection of individuals to put forward alternative views regardless of the accuracy or depth of their knowledge of the subject. The public are therefore exposed to apparent or actual real conflicts of information with the inevitable result that confusion reigns and effective action is hindered to a greater or lesser extent.

Biology vs medicine

To those of us from a scientific background the outcome of the campaign to deal with the pandemic has been surprisingly rapid and successful and credit is due to all those involved in the face of much media generated confusion. Since similar epidemics are always arising in one part of the world or another and largely unknown to the public in this country, it is obviously important to be alert and prepared. The history of medicine, especially in malaria has much to remind us of past mistakes. For example during the forty years of antislavery patrols off the coast of West Africa by the Royal Navy, there was considerable mortality from malaria and yellow fever despite many communications to the navy board from a variety of sources pointing out the connection between the arrival of mosquitoes and fevers. Those in charge took no action. Had they instructed ships captains simply to anchor their vessels further out to sea at night, the death rate of the crews could have been significantly reduced. Presumably those who wrote to the navy board about mosquitoes in the Victorian era did not write to the newspapers of the day or some notice of their letters might have resulted in worthwhile publicity and appropriate action.*

Closer to home, it was fortunate that the asbestos that was used to construct the huts in the Common Cold Research Unit would have been of the less dangerous type. The absence of a reply to my letter to the director raising the issue of asbestosis until after the air quality had been assessed, suggests that the authorities "had been caught on the hop". The absence of the word asbestos in Mr Thompson's book speaks for itself.

When the government enquiries into the corona pandemic begin their work, the inevitable question of preparedness and speed of response will come up. Assuming that my letter to the director of the Cold Unit was the first time anyone had thought about asbestos, why was this the first time that it had been questioned? As scientists we are driven by curiosity – as I was curious about the fact that there seemed to be this white dust over everything. Louis Pasteur's favourite saying is that "chance favours the prepared mind". By the phrase 'prepared mind' there is the implication of being alert and therefore becoming

---

* A memorial to those who participated in the campaign, in somewhat dilapidated condition, can be seen at the water's edge in Portsmouth not far from where Nelson departed these shores to join the HMS Victory

aware of novel situations which may include new diseases. We can ask if the training we give to those who want to study science or medicine is the most appropriate for these two disciplines.

While thinking about this problem I remembered the time I spent at Newcastle Medical School which had a different approach from traditional medical schools in that students were expected to learn by discovery for themselves, through early contact with patients rather than by listening to lectures (although they were given course notes). For a short time, I was asked to be a tutor to a small group of students who had to learn about the digestive system starting from scratch. When I asked what exactly I was supposed to do as a tutor I was told that my job was to act "as a midwife to the process of learning".* The idea from the beginning of this institution was that after qualification as General Practitioners as I understand it, they would continue this process of learning throughout their career. Which brings me back full circle to the theories of education which I should have learnt about and found rather boring, during my PGCE at Bristol.

As biologists we look at things with an evolutionary perspective – looking for genetic traits that affect survival either positively or negatively. This invites a broader perspective than only concentrating on individual anatomical systems to the exclusion of events in the rest of the body. We are more likely to look for general principals across a range of species. A typical example was Burkitt's observations that a single factor – that is the lack of dietary fibre – could be the cause of a range of ailments from heart attacks to varicose veins. More recently this would include the critical role of TNF that Ian Clark and colleagues have pursued. From my experience of working with

---

* I wasn't asked to do a second term obviously midwifery was not one of my talents!

Sydney Cohen, the background from which a medic views a problem is one that is strongly influenced by previous experience matched to text books and concentrating on a single condition (such as malaria) in isolation. Sydney's resistance to believing in antigenic variation was in contrast to someone with a biological training, as I had, who was quite ready to believe that such a mechanism could exist as a means of surviving immune responses of the host. Thinking with evolutionary principles as a viewpoint therefore encourages a process of lateral thinking. Whether the discovery approach of learning promoted at Newcastle Medical School helps GPs to think laterally to enable them to be more open and alert to new diseases, remains to be seen.

Personal Reflections

A big thank you

It is only on reflection, since I retired that I have come to realise that what I took as a routine job was almost unique in other peoples' eyes. I remember going to a Leverhulme Trust meeting in the 1960's when I had been working on malaria for a few months. All sorts of different disciplines (ballet dancers, doctors etc) were invited and I found myself standing next to a chap, very smartly dressed with a posh voice. For some reason I can't remember, he wanted to meet me for a breakfast meeting the following morning, but I couldn't do that as I said to him I had to take blood films from some monkeys. He said in a loud voice from across the hall "darling this man works on monkeys!" Perhaps if he had had a greater awareness of science he would not be so surprised that I was working on monkeys and would not need to inform his wife in quite such a public manner.

Some years ago on a tv advert Maureen Lipman, playing the part of a mother, tried to encourage her son, having passed only one exam "you got an 'ology, you're a scientist". I find it hard to believe that as a street kid from Fulham, I managed to get a few "'ologies" to work in a laboratory and write papers as a scientist. It just seems inherently unlikely considering my working-class background. There is no doubt of my great debt to my parents for supporting me through college, even though as I mentioned in the beginning, they didn't know the difference between a school and a medical school and my mother had no time for books. They could have refused to contribute and been more obstructive, pressurising me to get a "proper job". Further, I am especially grateful to Sydney Cohen for taking me on, setting me on the path to a scientific career. Considering we came from very different backgrounds we worked closely together for ten years and including my time at the London School and Porton, for a total of 18 years which I look back upon with immense pleasure. What is particularly poignant is that his son Roger Cohen, has written a book about their family history in which he describes with great courage and sensitivity, his mother's mental health problems, although those of us who worked closely with his father were totally unaware of these difficulties. I think this has only increased my admiration for Sydney.

I have a great awareness of my debt to my colleagues with whom I worked at Guy's, Imperial and the ANU, where work was not only immensely satisfying, but the people were an absolute pleasure to work with. There are too many other people both academics and technicians who helped me with my research over many years, though they may forget me, I shall never forget them.

Acknowledgements

Despite all the ups and downs, successes and failures, I hope we made a useful contribution to the science of malaria and although I may have mentioned them before I want to emphasise my profound thanks to all the people I worked with at Guy's: Graham Mitchell, Dave Dennis (deceased), Lawrie Bannister and Jean Langhorne. Also, the many young people who worked ably for us as technicians and went on to other careers, often in science and medicine.

I am also greatly indebted to Ian Clark at the ANU for his support and friendship and the enjoyment of working with him and benefitting from his vast knowledge of immunopathology.

I have the same sense of indebtedness to Bob Sinden who was also a good friend and it was a privilege to be a part of his team at Imperial College.

Not forgetting the wonderful time I had in Nigeria – it is a pleasure to see that one of my pupils is now a consultant at University College Hospital, Dr Olugbemiro Sodeinde. It is thanks to Paul King, my oldest friend, who encouraged me to go to Lagos, that my experience there was undoubtedly a turning point in my life.

Personally I would like to thank our many friends and neighbours who have supported us over the years and that we've managed to stay in contact with through all our wanderings. A special mention goes to artist Philip Castle – one of our oldest neighbours from our early Fulham days, who provided the picture of our beloved Ford Anglia.

Further thanks go to my grandson, another creative talent, Charlie Newhouse for the cover design of this book.

If having read this far and you were interested in furthering the cause of the fight against malaria, I would suggest a donation to the Royal Society for Tropical Medicine and Hygiene because of their internationally recognised teaching and research for many years, to which proceeds of this publication will be donated. I would also commend my son's charity, Techfugees, for helping refugees through the use of technology.

Lastly, this autobiography would never have seen the light of day without the devoted help of our daughter Helen. In addition to doing all the typing, editing and general organisation she has taken on the burden of dealing with the medical problems we both have, not to mention organising carers, taking me to doctors etc, and all of this through the complications of the pandemic. She has put aside her own interests as an artist with a unique talent and we could not have asked for more. We have so much to be thankful for, including our son-in-law Tim, who has also been a pillar of strength – thanks and love from Mum and Dad.

For Sue

Having written about my work colleagues it would be strange to say nothing about Sue, and our 55 years together but it is too personal to put much on to paper, that would be of much significance especially as she will not be reading this book.

Everyone who knows her, will recognise her in the cartoon by the work colleague when she left the maintenance department at the Royal Canberra Hospital. That sweet smile that comes from a warm personality that I have known so well is still there despite Alzheimer's. There are two little gems in my memory of which I can just about write, that not all our friends will remember. Firstly, although she loved being a teacher and anything to do with children the one job she really enjoyed out of all the others was being a court usher. She realised how some people coming to a court for the first time were extremely nervous, not knowing what to do or where to go or what would happen to them. She felt for them and did her best to calm their fears. Also the other part of the job was working with the judges and she really enjoyed this totally new experience which in a small way was a useful part of the legal system. She found the whole thing fascinating and it's a pity that she only did it for six years. As for our time together my other memory is from a journey back from Birmingham to London. We had been to the funeral of Professor Eric Ives. He was a good friend and guide to me when I was as a student and having a difficult time. As we got out of the train at Marylebone station and were looking for an exit, a young lady rushed up to us and said she had watched us talking all the way from Birmingham and just wanted to say she had never seen such love between two people. She rushed away leaving us stunned and unable to speak, it was such a lovely thing to do. What more can I say?

> "Man was made for joy and woe
> and when this we rightly know
> through the world we gladly go
> joy and pain are woven fine
> a clothing for the soul divine"
> **William Blake (1757-1827)**

Cartoon of Sue by Antonio Perez, 1988, one of 'The Maintenance Boys'

Bibliography

Burkett, D., *Don't forget fibre in your diet* (Collins 1979) ISBN 0-00-490020-0

Butcher, G. A., *Experimental Studies on Immunity to Plasmodium knowlesi* PhD, (University of London, 1970)

Butcher, G A, Malaria: *The Intelligent Traveller's Guide* (Australian National University, 1990) ISBN 0 86420 003x

Cohen, R., *The Girl From Human Street* (Vintage books, 2015) ISBN 978-0-307-74141-7

Cole, William ed., *The Fireside Book of Humorous Poetry* (Hamish Hamilton Ltd, 1965)

Dauncey, Elizabeth A., *Poisonous Plants* (Kew Publishing, 2010)

Defoe, Daniel, A *Tour Through the Whole Island of Great Britain* (Penguin, 1971)

Garner, Helen ed., *The New Oxford Book Of English Verse* (Oxford University Press, 1972) ISBN 0-19-812136-9

Garnham, P. C. C., *Malaria Parasites and Other Haemosporidia* (Blackwell, 1966)

Gilles, H. & Warrell, D. A., ed., *Bruce-Chwatt's Essential Malariology*, Third Edition (Edward Arnold, 1993) ISBN 0-340-57190-x

Gutteridge, M. C. & Halliwell, *Antioxidants in Nutrition Health and Disease* (Oxford University Press, 1994) ISBN 0 19 854902 4

Hardy, A. *The Spiritual Nature of Man* (Clarendon Press, 1979) ISBN 0-19-824732-X

Howse, E. N., *Saints in Politics,* (Open University, 1978) ISBN 004-942-088-5

Jackson, Brian., and Marsden, Dennis, *Education and the Working Class* (Pelican 1973)

Dictionary Of Quotations (The Oxford University Press, Second Edition, 1941) ISBN 0 907486959

Medawar, P. B., *Advice to a Young Scientist* (Pan Books, 1979) ISBN 0 330 26325 0

Muir, Frank, *A Kentish Lad* (Corgi, 1997) ISBN 0552-14137-2

Peechy, J., *The Whole Works of That Excellent Practical Physician Doctor Thomas Sydenham (*Corrected from the original Latin, DM.DCC.XVII, 1717)

Playfair, J., *Living with Germs.* (Oxford university press, 2004)

Pile, S., *The Book of Heroic Failures* (Routledge, Kegan, and Paul, 1979)

Root-Bernstein, Robert and Michele, *Honey, Mud, Maggots, and Other Medical Marvels: The Science Behind Folk Remedies* (Houghton Mifflin, 1997) ISBN 0 333 75038 1

Shaw, F. L., *A Tropical Dependency* (James Nesbit, 1905)

Thompson, K., *Harvard Hospital and Its Volunteers* (Danny Howell Books, 1991) ISBN 1 872818-04 8

Biography

This is a light-hearted account of forty years at the laboratory bench working on malaria with the ultimate aim of developing a vaccine. This involved much basic research on the need to understand this complex disease and its cause, including its interactions with other conditions. But this is not just about research as anyone who reads it will discover.

Born in London in 1940 at the beginning of the Blitz, Geoff Butcher was evacuated with his mother to Leicestershire to live with grandparents in Swannington, where they returned during school holidays after the war. They rejoined his father in 1944 to a small flat in Fulham. Having passed the eleven plus exam, Geoff went to Emanual school in Wandsworth and was supported financially by a State Scholarship later graduating with a BSc in Zoology from Kings College London in 1962. While taking a relaxing PGCE (Post Graduate Certificate in Education) course at Bristol University a friend teaching in Nigeria told him of a position to teach science in the Lagos Anglican Grammar School. There followed two wonderful years of interesting experiences. Deciding a teaching career was not for him, he worked as a Research Assistant on a vaccine against malaria; a collaboration between Prof Garnham at the London School of Hygiene and Tropical Medicine and Prof S Cohen at Guy's Hospital. He worked in various institutions: Microbiology Research Establishment, Porton Down; Newcastle

Medical School, Australia and the Australian National University, Canberra. All of this research was on malaria, funded by short term grants. He returned to the UK in 1990 to join a group at Imperial College, London. He has published over a hundred research papers spanning the immunology of malaria from *in vitro* culture to malaria transmission and vaccine testing and a guide for travellers and expatriates working for charities in malarial areas. Throughout his career and in retirement, he has written articles in defence of animal experimentation and about malaria for lay publications and lectured many lay groups such as schools, history groups and the U3A. His many interests outside of work encompassed emergency fostering, volunteering for Kew Gardens, trustee for Malaria Consortium and the Parkinson's Disease Society.

Lightning Source UK Ltd.
Milton Keynes UK
UKHW052024300522
403732UK00006B/351

9 781908 706430